Scottish Football

Requiem or Renaissance?

HENRY McLEISH

Luath Press Limited

EDINBURGH

www.luath.co.uk

First Published 2018

ISBN: 978-1-912147-59-5

The paper used in this book is recyclable. It is made from low chlorine pulps produced in a low energy, low emission manner from renewable forests.

Printed and bound by Bell & Bain Ltd., Glasgow

Typeset in 11 point Sabon by Lapiz

This book is dedicated to:
My grandfather, Henry Cunningham Baird: a thoughtful, Christian man,
socialist, mineworker and football player with East Fife in the years before
the start of WWI: my inspiration and also my source of football DNA.

The best football fans in the world who share my dream of a great
footballing country being able to once again achieve success on the
international stage.

Scotland's elite young footballers, a priceless asset in a world that
increasingly demands the highest level of skill and commitment.

Contents

Acknowledgements

I'D LIKE TO ACKNOWLEDGE my thoughtful friends and supportive family who have encouraged, listened and helped me with the ideas and themes in the book. A special word of thanks goes to Tom Brown, former political editor of the *Daily Record* for his ongoing advice and encouragement over many years of reflecting on Scottish life.

Introduction

SCOTTISH FOOTBALL IS CONTINUOUSLY under the microscope in what can appear to be an endless and relentless cycle of declining expectations, underachievement and underperformance on the field. Especially at international level, and where the game is challenged by history, institutional inertia and permanently insecure about its future. The game is fragmented and lacks direction and purpose. There seems to be no big ambition, no sense of sustained anger or urgency about the fact that a once spectacularly successful footballing nation, needn't be in this precarious and uninspiring place. A lack of brutal honesty at the heart of the game is preventing us from doing anything about it. This book rejects this dismal scenario that Scotland is destined to remain a second-rate footballing nation where the upper levels of European club competitions and the final stages of World Cups and European Championships are always beyond our reach. Instead, it argues that we should write a new and optimistic chapter in the remarkable history of our game.

For that to happen we must ask and answer searching questions about the mind-set of the game and look at structures, institutions, ethos and governance, culture and vision. Of significance and immediacy are the current levels of ambition for the Scotland team, as well as the question of purpose football serves in the modern era. This is about the anatomy of the game, what we can learn and how this can help shape the future. If Scotland is to build and maintain a competitive edge in club and international football, create a modern spectator sport, contribute to community and society and be part of the government's plans for a healthy and fit nation, lessons must be learned. Special, sectional, vested or narrow constituency interests must be confronted in order to build a broader and more sustainable model of what is in the best long-term interests of Scottish football.

The key to this is sustainable resources, attitude, building capacity to deal with change and for our institutions to have a much more open and transparent approach to new ideas and innovation: the game must reach out and embrace a wider Scotland. This is difficult. Our institutions are amongst the oldest in the world. The burden or legacy of history influences what we do, and how we think and act. For far too long there has been a reluctance to embrace modernity and make the game fit for purpose in the 21st century. My reviews of the game, commissioned by the SFA in 2010, were part of this process. There have been significant improvements since the reports were published but much more could, and should, have been done. Despite changes to structures and youth development, there has been little progress made in tackling institutional inertia, cultural constraints, an inward and insular attitude, deep-seated antagonisms and the unequal distribution of power and finance. These issues lie at the heart of the game's current decline.

The game remains fragmented and lacks coherence. There seems to be no bigger purpose than the day-to-day struggles – important though they may be – and no sense of a collegiate or collective endeavour. This could produce outcomes that would be more than the mere sum of the different parts of the SFA and SPFL. The fragile condition of the game is in constant need of fire-fighting and one that is out of step with the ideas and aspirations of a modern Scotland. This strikes at the heart of what change should mean. There is a great deal happening on a practical level involving skilled and committed professionals, and an extraordinary input of energy, emotion, and dedication from a vast army of fans, supporters, and other enthusiasts. But this is not seen as part of any big ambition or vision for the game, or a focus for the wider Scotland to rally around. What happens on the pitch, on the terraces and in the boardroom are vital parts of this long established game, but for the game to survive, be successful and be sustainable, a radical transformation is required in attitude and outlook. The game must reach out. This closed shop mentality deprives the game of ideas, inspiration and much needed allies. Football has to find its place in Scottish society and reconnect with mainstream thinking about where the nation is going. Too big to fail is one opinion, but too important to be left to its own devices is another.

There are big questions that need answered, but one thing is abundantly clear; football is too important to be left to the game alone! The game is reclusive and mistrusting. The game sees every critical friend as a critical enemy. There is a bewildering and corrosive atmosphere of cynicism, pessimism, and negativity surrounding it. This, of course, helps shape the defensive attitude of the game to the outside world. There is no greater sense of a better and bigger collective future than a game which could overcome the stifling sense of struggle and survival that many clubs experience day in, day out. Fans, the life blood of the game, feel their spending each match day is welcomed, but like voters between elections, they are not seen by the game as a valuable resource who could have much more to contribute. The game lacks strong and modern links with the world outside football. No game is an island. The valuable contribution football can make to a modern Scotland is currently limited by the attitude of the game and its unique and precious sense of its own importance which, in the eyes of the game, cannot be meddled with.

This book will:

1. Reflect on my own football journey, especially the early years in the game and the lessons learned. And, how the issues of identity, community, mining, religion, and class helped to shape my enduring interests, feelings, and passion for the game; helping to explain how an 'obsessive' is created: and seeing my world through a football!

2. Discuss the importance of football to Scotland and the indelible mark it has made on the national psyche – soul, mind and spirit – of the nation.

3. Examine the remarkable, even spectacular, history of the game in Scotland since 1873, the achievements at club level and the record breaking attendances which should be viewed today as an inspiring reminder of how, and why, we became a football loving nation; less about sentiment, nostalgia and, dare I say, delusion and more about DNA.

4. Spell out the role of football in the sporting life of the nation and how the game is such a fundamental part of the health, sport, fitness, and confidence building agenda that Scotland so desperately needs. This will touch on the relationship with government and with wider Scotland.

5. Review the issues and influences that have shaped the game over the last 30 years and identify when, why, and how football started to change, and to assess the consequences.

6. Consider the two major reviews of Scottish football undertaken in 2010 and reflect on the impact this has had on the game, the achievements since then and what the shortcomings have been.

7. Take an in-depth look at the governance of Scottish football, including the culture, the institutions, the mind-set, relationships, and the overall anatomy of the game today.

8. Work out why the game has become so disconnected from the world outside and how the game has become so defensive and dismissive of society playing its part in securing a better future and indeed shunning the very idea of the game being exposed to outside influence and criticism.

9. Learn lessons from Europe and the US about how modern football and sport is organised and governed. What does success look like and how do we create the conditions in Scotland for more innovation, more enterprise and ultimately more success?

10. Provide a blueprint for the transformation of Scottish football: how can we achieve a greater scrutiny, oversight, and regulation within the game through a shake-up of governance? To what extent should government get involved, as has been threatened by the Westminster Government in relation to the English FA? Is a single body required to run Scottish football in order to provide focus, parity of esteem between club and country and a more effective face to the outside world? Does the current league setup make sense, or is the lack of finance and the fear of change the only reasons for inaction? And, using a quote from another giant of the game, Jock Stein, 'Without fans who pay at the turnstile, football is nothing, sometimes we are inclined to forget that.' Is it not time for the fans to be represented at every level of the game and become a vital part of the modernisation of football?

This new book challenges and seeks solutions by looking into what can best be described as the anatomy, philosophy, politics and psychology of Scottish football. We need to understand the soul and spirit of this incredible sport, which has left such an indelible mark on our country for nearly 150 years. Through my own early experiences of football and, over a much longer period, my agonizing over the decline of the game, I am reminded of Bill Shankly's comment, 'of a game more important than life or death.'

Bedrock Principles for Common Sense Outcomes

We want to see a competitive, healthy and successful game which: **attracts** the widest possible levels of interest; **seeks** success at every level; **acknowledges** the importance of the game to every community in Scotland; is **aware** of the significant contribution football makes to the improvement of health, well-being and fitness of our nation; **aspires** to be a key part of a revolution in Scottish sport; **understands** the importance of the game for national pride and the Scotland brand; **delivers** financial success and sustainability; **values** the role the game plays in building character, respect, responsibility and confidence across all age groups, different social and economic needs and for both sexes; **routinely** participates in and qualifies for the final stages of European and World Cup tournaments at all levels and for both sexes; **continues** to seek success for the club game in Europe; **respects** and values the enormous contribution being made by fans, supporters and communities throughout Scotland; **accepts** that no game is an island unto itself and reaches out in a more inclusive and transparent manner to the wider Scotland; **takes** more responsibility for what happens within the game; **recognises,** in difficult financial times, that the game should not be dependent to the extent it is, on betting and gambling sponsorship, especially after society and then football have rejected the idea that cigarettes and alcohol should have a role in sport; **spells** out clearly its abhorrence of bigotry, sectarianism and racism in all its forms and in all locations.

Scottish football can be relevant, realistic, radical and rewarding, but to accomplish this we have to put in place an attitude of mind that lifts heads and seeks new horizons. The game needs to escape from its self-imposed retreat into fortress Hampden, increasingly isolated from critical thinking and an increasingly vocal Scotland wide fan base. The game seems curiously disconnected from the outside world. The club game will continue to tick over. For a supposedly football mad country this surely falls short of what we have experienced in the past or what we can hope for in the future. Let us stop selling ourselves short. Football can add value to country, club, and community, as part of a bigger ambition.

The following chapters, infused and enthused by my own football journey, attempt to explain how this can be done.

Let's be inspired and take note from the ambition of two of Scotland's greatest legends;

'We had a virus that infected everyone at United. It was called winning.'

- Sir Alex Ferguson

'At Manchester United, we strive for perfection. If we fail, we might just have to settle for excellence.'

- Sir Matt Busby

CHAPTER ONE

Parliament, Pulpit, Politics, Pride And The Queen

MUCH OF MY LIFE has been wrapped up in the game... an entire world in a football. If football means anything, it is about being rich in sentiment, nostalgia and brimming full of memories. At every turn in football these thoughts have been there, sometimes in a small way, sometimes looming large. But there is no doubt in my mind that the game cannot live off memories alone. So before making the case for a renaissance of the game, let's indulge ourselves a bit.

The Best Football Match in the World

The Real Madrid vs. Eintracht Frankfurt game, when Real won 7–3, has been recognised as the greatest game the world has ever seen. I was there in the crowd but my father, for some inexplicable reason, was sitting in the stand. There were 129,000 people there and what made the game so remarkable was that Eintracht had beaten Rangers 12–4, on aggregate, in the semi-final! Rangers at that time were also a great side. I can still name the Real team. It was like watching the Harlem Globe Trotters – there was nothing they couldn't do with a ball. Puskas and Di Stefano were scoring all the Real goals. The crowd was initially behind the German team but, by the end of the game, Real enjoyed one of most amazing receptions I have ever seen, so much so, they paraded the European Cup around the stadium to a tumultuous Hampden roar. Not one person left the game at the end of the match. Scotland and Hampden Park was a very special place for this kind of thing to happen.

In 2002, Real Madrid played in another European Cup final at Hampden Park and beat Bayern Leverkusena German side 2–1 in the final. Zinedine Zidane scored one of the greatest goals in world football and I was there to see it. After that, and reflecting on their great win in 1960, the Real team said, 'Glasgow belonged to them'; a fitting tribute from one of the greatest football teams in the World, to one of the truly great football cities of the world.

The 1960 win was just remarkable football, fantastic ball skills and gripping entertainment. They were just human beings, but nevertheless so talented and gifted. Football is a very simple game, played with the feet but guided by the brain. It shouldn't be so difficult to replicate!

Jock Stein

I met Jock Stein when I was playing with East Fife against Celtic reserves at Barrowfield in Glasgow in the mid-60s. This was a great honour. He was mingling with the young players as we had a pie and tea after the game. I'm sure he didn't need to be there on a dreich winters night, but he was. As a young player, there was no greater thrill than meeting one of the giants of your game.

Scotland Abroad

My first and last visit to watch Scotland play in the opening game of the World Cup was in 1998 in Paris, and a date which is now known as our infamous exit from the final stages of international tournaments, as well as a constant reminder of the fact that for 20 years since, our national game has been in decline. Craig Brown had a great run as Scotland manager after succeeding Andy Roxburgh. Both of them contributed to a remarkable run of qualifying for the finals of the World Cup; six times between 1974 and 1998, and reaching the final rounds of the European Championships in 1996 and 1998. This was the high watermark of Scottish international football achievement, reflecting a very different game in Scotland and a level of ambition and self-belief that, over 20 years, has faded along with the remarkable national sentiment and support, which there once was for the national game. My only consolation prize in Paris, was to meet Sean Connery at the game and lament on our defeat at the hands of the mighty Brazil. It would have been a more miserable discussion if we had been able to see into the future and realise that this was the to be the last time in 20 years that we would reach the final stages of any international tournament; a 'Scotland no more' moment.

Looking back on Paris, the visit may have been more significant than I had ever envisaged. My first great memory was leaving the Eurostar at the Gare Du Nord station on the day of the game. I couldn't believe my eyes. It was as if I had arrived in Queen Street station, Glasgow and exited onto George Square. But this was Paris. 'Here's tae us whas like us' was never truer. There were thousands of Scottish flags draped over everything and anything. I absorbed the scene with tears and immense pride. Scotland was here to do battle supported by the greatest football fans in the world and an incredible demonstration of national pride and patriotic fervour.

This was 1998 and 'The Scotland Act' was about to receive the Royal assent in autumn. I had been handling the passage of the Bill in the House of Commons. For the first time, in nearly 300 years, Scotland was one year away from having its own parliament in Edinburgh. It's always easy to read too much into events, but was this part of a massive transfer of football patriotism into political nationalism?; expressing national pride and patriotism, no longer on the badge on a blue football strip and the hallowed Hampden turf, but in a much more expansive embrace of political ambition for national recognition and identity. This wasn't the cause of our post–1998 decline, but since then, Scotland has changed. Our society is different and maybe interest, pride and sentiment in the game, has found other outlets.

I also think that our obsession with the importance of the international matches against England was ultimately a statement about the historic tensions and animosities between the two countries. It is worth remembering that these matches were played every year from 1872 until 1989. This was not healthy for Scotland. These games became more of an auld enemy distraction where victory over England became a short-term morale boost, and not the best way to measure our performance as a footballing nation. Rerunning the battle of Culloden didn't have much appeal for me. Perhaps the expressed dislike of the English, sometimes fun and sometimes deadly serious, was swallowed up instead, as part of the nationalism and populism of the devolution years.

Faith and the Fans

My first visit to Hampden Park was in 1955 when I was seven years of age. It was with my grandfather to see Billy Graham, the famous American Evangelist. I have few recollections of the religiosity of the occasion but remember vividly, the awesome size of the stadium and the atmosphere of the crowd. In my early years, religion and football had many encounters and it was always strange to think that my grandfather and I shared the same club, and that I eventually played in the same position on the park, 57 years apart!

My Old Club, Better Days

My old club has had a remarkable history. East Fife won the Scottish League Cup three times in four years during the late '40s, and was one of only two clubs from the second tier of Scottish football to win the Scottish Cup. Their remarkable Scottish cup run attracted an astonishing 400,000 fans. Using current home game attendances at Bayview each season, the club would need 45 years to attract a comparable figure. How times have changed. But this is what is inspiring about the game; club achievement, history, pride, identity, commitment, loyalty, passion and often an affection that trickles down the years. Six special train-loads of East Fife supporters were amongst the 97,710 fans at Hampden on the Wednesday night replay.

When I was a young player with East Fife, I had tea in Paisley with John Sneddon, who was the club captain when they lifted the trophy at Hampden. The meeting was arranged by East Fife's manager, Jimmy Bonthrone. What a privilege it was to see and handle the medal that he had won and worn on that night when they arrived back with the cup to an ecstatic welcome in Methil. My grandparents were there, cheering and soaking up what must have been an incredible atmosphere. My legacy from that night was two very thin tumblers with the result and team name inscribed on them, which were passed down to me by grandparents.

Best Player Ever

Watching on television, 17-year-old Pele play for the first time was also a great inspiration. In the final of the World Cup in 1958, Brazil defeated home nation Sweden 5-2, and Pele scored twice. Once again, incredible skills were on display and I was just in awe of the intricacies of passing, spectacular individual ball skills and the speed and decisiveness of wave after wave of attacking football. This was a new era unfolding with Pele and the Brazilians continuing to dominate world football and the World Cup.

Her Majesty the Queen

Public service and politics have given me unparalleled opportunities to visit places and meet people, a lot of which I would not have been able to do in normal jobs. In this context, meeting Her Majesty the Queen was both a privilege and a remarkable experience. The queen is a fascinating person to meet; Head of State, monarch, diplomat and skilled politician, with wisdom that reflects her long period in office and experiences that are probably unique in world affairs. I have met her on a number of occasions, as a minister and as First Minister.

Prime Ministers and First Ministers are invited to Balmoral to spend a night and have dinner. For a working-class boy from Methil, this scenario was, to put it mildly, daunting and challenging. This sets the scene in 2001 when my wife and I were invited to visit. Leaving aside much of the evening's activities, the dinner became focussed on football. I was sitting beside the Queen at dinner with Sophie Wessex on my other side. Not long into the dinner my pager – no sophisticated iPhones or other digital devices at that time – went off. I just ignored it so as not to cause embarrassment or inconvenience to Her Majesty, but it just kept buzzing and I kept ignoring it. Eventually her Majesty leaned over and said, 'I think that is your pager'. I thanked her and kept ignoring it. Leaning over again she said, 'I think you should answer and find out what it is'. So I came clean and said that Scotland were playing Belgium in a World Cup qualifier and my staff have been trying to get the scores. This having failed, she said, 'Philip scores, please'. The prince then asks one of the butlers to get the scores. Some minutes later, he returned. He said, 'Maam, there is good news and bad news, England won but Scotland lost." Content, but sad that Scotland wouldn't be going on to the finals, I resumed my meal. I hoped this was the end of the story, but the Queen had one final comment up her sleeve. After a few more minutes of eating, she leaned over again and said, 'Well First Minister, that's just the way it goes!' Once again, the beautiful game had intervened but mercifully hadn't caused too many royal waves. The queen was calm and gracious, and I was just pleased and relieved to have arrived at the point in the dinner where I could retire and sip a whisky with the Duke of Edinburgh. I did not dare ask the queen if she had any interest in football.

Pope John Paul II

Good cartoonists are worth their weight in gold. In 2000, I received an invitation to go to Rome with Secretary of State, John Reid and Cardinal Winning to celebrate the 400th anniversary of the Scots College in Rome. We had an audience with Pope John Paul II at the Vatican. I am not a member of any faith or church but I do have enormous respect for such a remarkable church leader and world statesman.

Being in the Vatican, hearing him reply to young people representing the United Nations and speaking in 15 different languages was not just a privilege but also an extraordinary example of presence and towering humility. In his presence you sensed that this was one of the most significant figures of modern times and a great leader. It was invigorating and inspiring. Though I was not aware of it at the time, this was a small piece of history because it was the first time that the head of the Scottish Government had met the Pontiff since the reformation 500 years before.

Some years after this visit, I was in and about Hampden conducting my review of Scottish football for the SFA, when I noticed a cartoon on one of walls near the downstairs café. It was very funny and gave a commentary on my personal audience with the Pope. His holiness is in his splendid papal chair and I am bending with his hand clasped in mine. The caption shows the Pope saying to me, 'Delighted to meet you First Minister, but I am a bit worried about the state of your old football team, East Fife'. Once again, when you're associated with football, it goes everywhere with you. John Reid is, of course, a Celtic fan and past Chairman of the Club, so he had no such problems with Pope John Paul II: our press can be both creative and funny!

Politicians and Football

You can sometimes tell if a politician is interested in football from the way they read their newspapers; from back to front! This was certainly the case in the tea-room of the House of Commons where many MPs (mainly Scottish) would often combine eating an unhealthy, but noble, bacon roll with a perusal of the latest football news. Gordon Brown and the late Donald Dewar were students of the game and were back-to-front readers. They were very knowledgeable about the game, often surprisingly so.

Gordon Brown figures prominently in my recollections of football and politics. Before the World Cup in 1990, Scotland was involved in qualifying matches and as a group of Scottish MPs at Westminster, we were keen to watch the Scottish matches being televised. Much to our annoyance, one of our games was being televised in Scotland but not in London. It was disappointment all around until Gordon Brown pulled of a miracle. The live feed for the game was only going to Scotland direct from Europe, but with the help of his brothers in the media, he was able to get the broadcasting feed directed into the House of Commons. It therefore became the only place in the UK, outside of Scotland, where this game could be seen. All of the Scottish MPs, and even some English MPs, could watch the game in one of the committee rooms with wine, beer and sandwiches thrown in.

Politics, football and community have always been linked in all parts of Scotland. Not surprising then that in the years before devolution, our national game should still be an important part of our life at Westminster where passion, patriotism and pride in the game were as strong as in any part of Scotland.

This next sport and football story starts in Kirkcaldy. Early one Saturday morning I received a phone call from Gordon Brown. He asked if Caryn, my wife, and I would like to join him in Kirkcaldy and meet some American friends from Harvard University. We accepted and arrived at the Beveridge Hotel, Kirkcaldy, near to lunchtime. As soon as we arrived, Gordon suggested that he and I jump into his car, complete with security detachment, and drive to Cowdenbeath. The club had been promoted and there was to be a photo call as the new league flag was unfurled on the pitch. This was a whirlwind tour at break-neck speed including photos, fans, club directors and tea. This was a chance for Gordon to share in a great day for the fans in a former mining community, one which had seen better and more prosperous days but still had a great community spirit and sense of solidarity, of which football was a vital part. We headed back to Kirkcaldy but, little did I know, the day was only starting!

The former Prime Minister and Chancellor, after arriving back in Kirkcaldy, asked me if I had any ideas about where he could take his friends so they could see something of Fife. I was informed they were only here for a few hours so I came up with the idea that we pile into the two Range Rovers with security and escort, and head to St Andrews and the Old Course Hotel where, from the fourth floor Road Hole lounge, there are magnificent views of the Old Course, the home of golf and an iconic point of pilgrimage for all Americans. Sitting in the lounge at the Old Course, I thought mission accomplished but this wasn't the end.

One of Gordon's friends had a slowly unfolding but inspirational idea. She commented on the fact that the film, *Chariots of Fire*, had been filmed on the sands of St. Andrews and suggested a visit. We piled back into our transport and drove to the sands. At this point, my wife decided to stay with the security detail and so Gordon, his friends and myself braced ourselves for a walk along the sands. His friend's wife then suggested we run, albeit at a slow pace, along part of the sands. This was challenging enough but then she insisted that I whistle the *Chariots of Fire* theme as we ran along the golden sands! Of course, I agreed and the scene was surreal. The four of us ran along the sands for a few hundred yards accompanied by my special rendering of the whistling version of 'Chariots of Fire', never performed anywhere in the free world and hopefully not being viewed, or listened to, by any human being on this stretch of beautiful Fife coastline. Our guests were delighted and Gordon was intrigued. I was musing about my first solo whistling record contract from this unique performance.

Now for the post-script. I was hoping against hope that no one had witnessed our adventure. It was a cold day and the beach appeared to be deserted with few signs of life behind the sand-dunes. The next day, a phone call from the *Daily Record* diminished my faith in human nature. The reporter curiously inquired as to whether the former Prime Minister and First Minister had taken leave of their senses, or had it just been a remarkable piece of publicity seeking. I assured him that neither was true. We laughed and I said it was just a spectacular and enjoyable piece of fun, and so it was. We had been spotted by a family from Lanarkshire who had understandably passed it on to the Record. Predictably, but in a sympathetic and funny depiction, the Record had a page three spread showing Dr Brown and I, dressed in Olympic athletics gear, burning the calories on the famous beach. The fact that so many people watched the film and remember the location it was filmed, is a great tribute to the real star, Eric Liddell, and to Scotland.

On a sadder note, Gordon Brown and I attended the funeral of one of Scotland's famous footballing sons, Jim Baxter in Glasgow. Born in Hill of Beath, Fife, Jim played for Raith Rovers before joining Rangers, and died in 2001. The family had asked us to attend and I was privileged and honoured to pay my respects to one of Scotland's greatest talents. Sitting in the Cathedral in Glasgow, it was easy to remember his finest hour against the 'auld enemy' at Wembley in 1967, when Scotland beat the world champions. Jim, with a breathtaking display of bravado and skill, tortured England, including Nobby Stiles (the hard man of all hard men) and gave a personal and brilliant interpretation of the beautiful game. A statue honouring Jim Baxter was unveiled in 2003, just a few yards from where he started to play. At the ceremony Gordon Brown described him as having played with, 'authority, athleticism and majesty'. Nobody has said it better.

Glory in Dublin

Despite the warring factions in politics and our love of tribalism, our Holyrood Parliament has another side to it, an all-party football team. Enough cooperation existed to put together a team and a particularly memorable game for me was when we played the Dail Eireann, the Irish Parliament, in Dublin in 2002. This was an international match that ended in a draw and was conducted in a tough, but good-natured, Celtic way. I had always envisaged a bigger role for Scotland on the world stage, though I never envisaged the Scottish parliamentary football team as being one of my priorities to further that aim!

I was thrilled, in my mid-fifties, to receive the man of the match award: I was merely content to stand up after the last ball had been kicked. My teammates were indulging me in some sentiment and nostalgia, and for my past services to the beautiful game. I was grateful for their gesture but in truth, the man of the match should have been Tommy Sheridan. While totally at odds with his politics, I was impressed with his skills, energy, and strength in mid-field where we partnered up. The Holyrood team was also packed out with other world-class stars such as Dennis Canavan, Kenny MacAskill and now Presiding Officer, Ken Macintosh.

The Guinness Brewery in Dublin was the venue for our post-match reception, with no complaints from anyone. Ireland is a fascinating country with a great sense of history and now, modernity. There is also less material-ism with a much more spiritual make-up, and as a nation, they have a much soul, which we can learn from. It is also worth reminding ourselves of their recent international football history, which has eclipsed Scotland's lack of achievement. But again, their population is smaller than ours. These com-parisons with other smaller countries speak volumes about our decline on the international stage. Accepting the fact that their league structure bears no comparison to ours, is it a benefit that they have no competing priori-ties to the tasks of finding young Irish talent and investing both spirit, and finance, into their international game?

The problems of Scottish football may manifest themselves on the pitch at Hampden and at 42 other club venues throughout Scotland, but they don't start there. Instead, Scotland's problems are concentrated in the insti-tutions, the culture and out-dated mind-sets of a game that increasingly looks inward for solace and inspiration and, in doing so, is cutting itself off from the very people that can help breathe new life into it. It is about ambition. It is about our DNA. It is about self-belief. It is about wakening up to what small population countries – Ireland, Northern Ireland, Wales and Iceland – with wider horizons are telling us, year after year after year.

Disaster at Wembley

Westminster also has a football team comprising members of the House of Com-mons and yes, the House of Lords. One of our first matches, in the late 1980s, was held at Crystal Palace's ground at Selhurst Park, on one of the very early all-weather pitches. Tackling was a nightmare. It was like playing on a Brillo pad. So after a few tackles and chunks of skin lying around, I quickly realised that ducking physical contact and staying on my feet was the only way to survive. Thankfully our modern three and four G pitches are more player-friendly.

My greatest and most painful recollection was when we played at the home of English football, Wembley Stadium, against the press or lobby correspondents from the parliament. I always dreamed of playing at Wembley and this was my opportunity, although playing against newspaper men was a bit of a let down. On the bright side, it was maybe an opportunity to settle old scores with journalists who had been harshly critical of me.

We were first in the famous dressing rooms, then we walked up the tunnel where the ground staff had kindly turned on the recording of the Wembley roar (a whimper compared with ours at Hampden) and we entered the great empty stadium. Without being insulting to England, I could only think of that memorable day in 1967 when we beat the world champions and Jim Baxter had the time of his life.

But then disaster hit. Not long into the game, I was injured and had to be carried off the hallowed turf. My mind was trying to process how this could be and I thought, 'why me?' I was probably the only person having the time of his life as an ex-professional and football obsessive. It provided a good laugh for my parliamentary colleagues and much merriment amongst the press corp. The next day, the *Daily Mirror* had a piece and three photographs detailing my misfortune, which was both funny and sympathetic:

> Some people think it's all over... it is now. Football is a funny old game. One minute, Glenrothes MP was in full flight as a team from the House of Commons took on the press at Wembley Stadium. The next, the former East Fife star was being helped from the pitch by some of his Parliamentary colleagues after straining a muscle. The MPs lost the game 4-2 but Henry said, 'It was an unforgettable experience playing on the famous turf.'

I was conscious that as politician and a Scot in a pickle amidst the hostile environs of England's home of football, my press colleagues would live off that for a long time. The game at Wembley did bring a human face to the usually savage and unforgiving world of Westminster. Football has that reach.

Disaster and Tragedy

I remember as if it was yesterday, the Munich air disaster of the 6th of February 1958, when 23 people died. Many of the Manchester United first team, including the brilliant young player, Duncan Edwards, whose full potential had still to be realised, where sadly lost. Sitting in my bedroom aged ten, on that cold winters night, the news came over the radio and I felt heart broken and sad that people in my world of football had so tragically died. I have remained interested in the club ever since and there has always been a sentimental attachment, reinforced by the Scottish dimension of outstanding managers, Matt Busby and Alex Ferguson.

Football is, of course, a hugely emotional and sentimental game, filled with memories and dreams but often tragedies and grief too. There have been more disasters in football than in any other sport. It is the most popular sport on the planet and will have therefore have its share of tragic events, but the horrific nature of some of them does mark football out.

On 29 May 1985 at the Heysel Stadium in Brussels, 39 people lost their lives and 600 were injured when a riot took place involving Juventus and Liverpool fans. On 15 April 1989 at Hillsborough, 96 people lost their lives and 766 were injured during a semi-final of the FA cup between Liverpool and Nottingham Forrest. On 11 May 1985 at Bradford, 56 people lost their lives and 250 were injured during a match between Bradford City and Lincoln City.

Closer to home on the 2nd of January 1971, 66 people lost their lives and more than 200 were injured during a match between Rangers and Celtic. Stairway 13 collapsed and a number of fans were crushed to death. The first disaster at Ibrox occurred during a 1902 home-international between Scotland and England, when 25 people lost their lives and 517 were injured.

Football has experienced many tragedies and the only silver lining in many of those dark cloudy days, is the push it gave to better conditions for the fans, providing a demand for all seated stadia and the recognition that, while there had been great improvements on the pitch, not enough had been done for fan comfort, convenience and safety. Since the end of the 1980s, there has been a greater recognition of the importance of fans and their need for safe surroundings, but more must be done. Fans are the life-blood of the game. Their role as fans goes alongside their financing of the game as customers and we should never forget the history and solidarity that they pass from one generation to the next, keeping the game alive and relevant.

On the Ball

Achieving First Minister of Scotland is one thing but being a guest on *Off the Ball*, hosted by Stuart Cosgrove and Tam Cowan, felt like my finest hour. The iconic, irreverent, funny, outrageous yet right-on-the-money BBC programme has hosted me three times. The first, and funniest, was when I was First Minister nearly 20 years ago. Tam Cowan was keen to explore my 'keepie-uppie' record, so he produced a football and asked me if I would perform on the programme.

The only problem was the fact that this was a radio programme and nobody would see it happening. However, that wasn't a problem for Tam and so I took the ball, went into a corner of the studio and performed! Listeners would only hear the sporadic bounces of the ball in the background as Tam and Stuart continued their banter. After what seemed an interminable time in the corner, they put me out of my self-imposed exile and I returned to join them. What a politician will do to court popularity!

The programme's brilliance lays in its ability to reflect the humanity and frailty of the game, as well as the humour, the passion and the 'heres tae us whas like us' attitude of the game to the outside world. Football needs this, the constant reminder of the Bill Shankly strain of political thinking, that football is more important than life or death.

Elite Talent

Cristiano Ronaldo stands out in my memory. During my visit to his academy, Sporting Lisbon in Portugal, as well as my visit to the Bernabeu Stadium, home of Real Madrid, to see Liverpool play in the European Cup, his strength in his dedication to the cause was obvious. He understands the level of national support that young players need to succeed. Ronaldo had a ball attached to his feet for the period he spent at the Academy.

East Fife on Fire

On this night, the club were away to Stranraer, with an overnight stay in Girvan, Ayrshire. At midnight, a staff member started a fire and all the players had to escape. It was very dangerous and serious. But the next morning came and the game had to go on. However, in order to get there, the Chairman of the Club, Big Jock Fleming, had to take most of the players to Marks and Spencer to buy them sweaters and trousers as their clothes had been burnt in the fire. On a dark and damp day in Stranraer, we lost the match, but certainly returned home with a story to tell.

Giants of the Game and Great People

Jimmy Johnstone, Billy McNeil, Tommy Gemmell, Sandy Jardine, Ally McCoist and John Greig: giants of the game with an ordinary touch. They were a credit to club and country and they played for the love of both. Relative to their time, the attendances that they attracted and the tons of respect they had in their local areas and within their fan base, their financial rewards were not great and certainly nothing in comparison to their contemporaries. They were ordinary humans with extraordinary skill, talent and humility.

Chair of the Fife Elite Academy

In my review of Scottish football in 2010, I recommended the organisation of a new youth strategy and the creation of youth academies throughout Scotland. I now chair the Fife Academy comprising of the four Fife Clubs; Dunfermline, Raith Rovers, East Fife and Cowdenbeath. This has provided me with invaluable insights into both the potential and the problems, which face our children and young people in building a future in the game. Scotland is not yet in the right place and the tensions between club and country, SPFL and SFA, and the unfair and unequal distribution of power and money within the game is seriously holding us back. It is meanwhile allowing other countries to march forward as we collectively fail to understand the enormity of our youth crisis and stubbornly refuse, or are unable to see, the bigger global picture. My time in the role of chairing the academy has brought many issues to my attention: we have a broken youth player pathway, serious underfunding, no incentives for clubs to think young, too many mediocre foreign players, too much short-termism, unbalanced investment, no big ambition and a failure to understand or grasp the demands from our country for success.

CHAPTER TWO

Football: An Aspiration Gap

A CURSORY ANALYSIS OF Scottish football reveals a game overwhelmed by significant strains or tensions. First, the self-interest of few clubs seeking success, now at odds with the many who see survival as their goal. To be fair, some would argue that this might be inescapable if we are to have club sides competing in Europe. Second, the decline of our national side may be the result of the battle between club and country. Third, the increasingly intense power struggles within the headquarters at Hampden are a takeover, in all but name, of the SFA by the SPFL. This has enormous implications for the national game. There is an important argument to be had about the governance of the game in Scotland. But this should be the product of a root and branch debate about ambition, direction and purpose and not just as a by-product of the imbalances and unfairness in the current distribution of power and finance in the Scottish game. Fourth, the current distribution of power, status, authority, finance, and opportunity within the game are having both intended and unintended consequences, which are undermining the national game in Scotland and the prospects for our international team. Fifth, since my review of youth and elite talent in 2010, we are still struggling to put together a coherent, innovative and state-of-the-art academy system for children and young people. Nearly a decade on, we are still discussing structures and failing to radically transform our offering to our talented youngsters, or to seriously acknowledge that the future of Scottish football is home grown talent. This is fast becoming a missed opportunity as the original ideas are being watered down, the big ambition is being dismantled, the distribution of funding is being distorted meaning that much of Scotland will be left without adequate access to the resources desperately needed to find, nurture and deliver our precious talent.

Once again, some of the clubs are in danger of sacrificing the national and international game for narrow self-interest. For 20 years Scotland has not qualified for the final stages of the European Championships or the World Cup. It is a logical and convincing argument to suggest that elite development at club level has not served our international interests. So why are we seeing a disproportionate amount of national game finances still flowing their way when outcomes have been poor and other parts of Scotland, and many of the clubs in league football, are being starved of resources? Talent exists every-where in Scotland and we are wasting money and time if we ignore this basic truth of football life. Our international prospects have not been served well by low ambition, and this rapidly intensifying clash between club and country.

The decisive factor in any struggle to transform football is the low level of ambition, which now stalks and shapes the Scottish game. This explains our underachieving and underperforming, not only in football, but in other aspects of Scottish life. Despite this, my views are based on a remarkably optimistic view of Scotland's footballing future. My main arguments or jus-tification for my optimism are based on five key considerations.

First, acknowledging the dramatic social, economic, cultural, and polit-ical changes in post-war Scotland and the impact of issues such as class, identity and religion. Also, the incidence of poverty and inequality; there are a variety of other factors that must be factored in to any analysis of our game. These changes are not unique to Scotland, but the extent of the decline in our game is, especially at international level. The last 30 years have been dramatic and raise the question of why Scotland has experienced such a drastic and dismal decline, and crucially what other 'Scottish' factors have been at work. Our excuses are legendary. There is the idea that our children and young people now have other things to occupy themselves, including the onslaught of the hi-tech, Facebook society and the much talked about fact that there is not so much poverty around to inspire and enthuse them. But other countries haven't maintained poverty levels artificially high, or banned children from the digital age in order to maintain good national sides! Our arguments lack credibility and are the refuge of the despairing and the desperate, and only provide reassuring comfort for the complacent and for those who refuse to own up to a lack of ambition. But on a comparative basis none of this makes much sense. Stripping away many layers of excuses exposes the more credible idea of our decline being linked to our collective failure as a footballing nation, to understand change, our defensive and lim-ited response to these changes and instead, to seek shelter in a low ambition, high victimhood environment. Other countries have just done better than us. We always have choices. Maybe our decline was made in Scotland.

Second, there is no doubt that as some countries have declined, other new and emerging countries, at both club and national level, without old ways and less football baggage, have seized their opportunity and won football success. Some have developed good national sides but have made limited impact at club level. Again, this raises questions about Scotland. Are we being too ambitious in seeking success at both club and country level? How do you succeed at both? Is the way we play our game out-dated? Why did we not see this coming? Why does our game learn very few lessons from other countries, new and old? Is our insularity a problem? Is a remarkable football history a blessing, or a curse? It is not the fault of our new international competitors that they have moved forward, and we have regressed or at least stalled? Maybe our failure to understand and respond to change was made in Scotland.

Third; the Iceland phenomenon. This raises the question of how a country, that is half the size of Glasgow, has created a football revolution and qualified for the European Championships in 2016, and the World Cup in 2018. Structured, composed, disciplined, and focused football has been built on a modern technical approach, ruthless levels of fitness, state of the art facilities (including indoor) and an aggressive approach to winning international success. These qualities are not found at the end of rainbows or made in heaven, or the product of poor children playing football on ice covered streets in the middle of Reykjavik. The level of ambition and national pride is a driver of success. Iceland is important because it removes any semblance of victimhood that we may wish to deploy to defend our international performances over at least the last 20 years. Our failure to modernise our game, innovate and raise our level of ambition was made in Scotland.

Fourth, we must consider the importance of football to Scotland and the indelible mark it has made on the soul of the country. This is more than sentiment, delusion, or nostalgia. This is about the DNA of Scottish football, and raises the question of what ever happened to it. Adam Smith, a very famous Scot, wrote *The Wealth of Nations*. Borrowing some of his ideas, let's describe the talent of children and young people, of both sexes, as the 'wealth of football' and the basis of the long term 'common good' of the game. There is nothing to suggest that the DNA of football genius is still not out there in every part of Scotland. There is a difference between talent, the golden threads of the tapestry of the game, existing in every part of Scotland and, on the other hand, our failed efforts to find, value, and nurture this precious resource and then providing the opportunity for our young players to serve club and country. Who can say that talent doesn't exist in Scotland to the same extent it existed before? Maybe the talent that underpinned the golden football decades of the post-war period is still there but our limited success in developing it has not been as successful or consistent as it might have been. In many ways, this is a gross understatement of the truth. We have let our young people down. This is a 'made in Scotland' issue. What we do with our most important football resource is our responsibility; no one else is to blame.

Finally, the decline of Scottish football did not happen overnight. There was no big bang or one single dramatic intervention that left the game reeling and embarking on a spiral of decline. Indeed, it is often said that in the last few years, club attendances have propelled Scotland to having the highest per capita club attendances within UEFA. This is an important point. It is worth acknowledging, however, that a country with a small population, and two clubs with a combined average attendance of 100,000 fans, does tend to distort the per-head of population calculations. But, as the narrative will show, there have been an extraordinary number of issues, changes, ideas, and events that have, over time, impacted the game, and resulted in profound and often unforeseen consequences. The current state of the game benefits the significant few at the expense of the many and has had a hugely detrimental effect on the national game, our international performance and the status and appeal of the game in the hearts and minds of wider Scotland.

Understanding change allows us to dig deeper in our search for solutions to existing problems and help create a new template for the future. There is nothing that is inevitable about the direction of Scottish football, but any change must be rooted in an understanding of how we got here, why we are here, what are the big issues and where do we want to be.

Politics of Inevitability

The politics of inevitability need not apply, but the longer our current situation survives, the more difficult change will become as other countries continue to push ahead and failure on our part is more exposed. No one is any doubt about the significance of finance and its distribution, the media, the power structure within the game, the lack of transparency and democracy, television rights, our growing dependence on foreign players and our near total reliance on betting, as a financial sponsor. Much of this has led to the game being diminished in the eyes of many, but on the other hand, there are supporters of the inevitability of current trends, mainly the beneficiaries of the current structure who are content to embrace so called 'realism' and who reject a transformation of the current game. It is of course understandable that our big clubs should be concerned about their ability to compete in Europe, and to be critical of any changes that would lessen their control and authority within the game and undermine their financial stability. But they should also accept that this strategy has consequences and that their success should not be at the expense of our total game, further improvements to our league set up or drastically improved performances on the international stage. Too high a price may have already been exacted. A new future for the game can be made in Scotland.

These are five powerful reasons for being optimistic. The world of football has changed and so has every aspect of our lives and society, but this is more than just a game. We must escape from the narrow confines of traditional thinking and the constraints that the game has imposed upon itself. We need to learn and be wise to the success of others. We need to reach out from, what I believe to be, a self-imposed isolation and become a new, dynamic, modern game fired by a bigger ambition and a clear vision which is built on the outstanding history of the Scottish game and the undoubted potential which DNA has bequeathed to us. We have choices to make.

Finding a Way Back

Vision is a difficult word, but as far as Scottish football is concerned, the immediate shape of it seems obvious and uncomplicated. There must be regular participation by the national team in the final stages of international tournaments. There should be a prosperous professional sector with clubs being financially secure and achieving well above the country's population size in international club competitions. The UEFA and FIFA regimes of country and club coefficients are brutal and unforgiving. The further you fall, the harder it is to recover. Our aim must be for Scotland to be recognised by other football associations as a shining beacon of the best practice in modern football – currently we are not – and in football governance. Scottish elite talent should be regarded as top-class players around the world and sought by the best clubs in Scotland and Europe. All Scottish young people must have the opportunity to be coached by the best and play football in high quality facilities, at least equal to the best of other western European countries. There must also be a revolution in the way we treat fans, in how we improve their experience of football and involve them in all aspects of the game. This is what a definition of success might look like.

The failure to qualify for the 2018 World cup had a significant and symbolic impact on the game and on our already deflated sense of national pride and confidence, continuing as it did the ongoing sense of failure that has lived with us since Paris, 1998. The psychological damage of this and the prospect of further failures has once again reignited interest into the longest running inquest in European Football. In a much more dramatic and characteristically pointed fashion, the fans and those who care about the game are asking 'WTF' has happened to Scottish football. My book is intended to answer that question and provide a way forward.

Troubled and turbulent times have exposed, once again, a game in need of radical reforms that are aimed at:

- Transforming its weak, non-transparent and out-dated governance

- Accelerating the modernisation of structures and institutions

- Setting in place more effective relationships with the world outside football

- Building new relationships with fans and supporters, and widening and diversifying the fan base

- Establishing a bigger ambition and a more enlightened vision

- Changing institutions and culture

- Rebalancing the distribution of power, finance, authority and opportunity within the game and, in particular, between club and country, and the SFA and the SPFL

- And, getting the wealth of our game (talent) right

It is reassuring to think that Scottish football has not always been as tormented and troubled. Today, there are so many warring factions in and around the game, a constant deluge of criticism, and competing and often contradictory opinions about what the game needs and yet, very little evidence of what lies behind our problems. But two factors give us an insight into the crisis facing the game. First, there is an underwhelming level of collective ambition in the corridors of power at Hampden, giving the impression that doing and delivery leave little room for reflection and reality checks. At the heart of the game there is little real democracy and while we talk about 'membership organisations', the reality is very different as any real power and influence is wielded by the few, not the many, and as stated earlier, the national and international game does not have the prominence it needs to be successful. Second, the increasingly isolated nature of the governing bodies running the game in Scotland are creating real tensions between themselves and the outside world of organisations that wish to help and improve the game. Government is a classic example of an institution that wants to help but is increasingly frustrated in their intentions by the inward-looking nature of the game, the circling of the wagons with 'keep out' notices which become prominent when the game doesn't warm to the ideas of the wider society, and when the game is offended by being asked to assume more responsibility for what, are essentially, football matters: there is often a simmering resentment.

The fragile and fraught nature of the current game, the prominent role it still has in Scottish society, the enormous goodwill of the long-suffering fans and the genuine interest that 'obsessives' like myself have in seeing a football renaissance, provide a basis for optimism and the prospect of achieving success.

Success and Achievement

A dip into the history of the game reveals a sensational past with a remarkable record of success and achievement. A small, cold-climate country on the edge of Europe has produced players, clubs and international teams that were the envy of the world and a source of unprecedented pride and passion in Scotland. We remain the only country in the world to retain record-breaking club and international football attendances. Punching above our weight was a successful, national past-time. But this is also a story of how this success dramatically faded and for reasons that are difficult, on the surface, to understand. Scottish football entered a dark period of retreat from the final stages of the World Cup and European Championships and, at club level, made little impact in Europe. Why did this happen and what were the factors in the 1980s and 1990s that changed the nature of the game, undermined our confidence, and destroyed the sparkle that success can bring to both game and nation?

Decline and Success

These significant changes are still being felt today as the fragile condition of the game raises questions about the future of football. We need to look at the ideas of decline and success. Put simply, decline is a gradual and continuous loss of strength, quality and value – not just to the game itself but also to others – and to diminish and deteriorate. But if you are part of the game, it is difficult to recognise the symptoms as there is no single event that stands out and all the changes just become part of the 'ups and downs' of the game, maybe uncomfortable and unacceptable, but not life threatening or particularly noteworthy. In the absence of strategic nous, decline is a path that is easily trodden as the cumulative impact of change goes unnoticed and reaches a point where it is too difficult to do anything. A new normal arrives and is quickly adjusted to. This helps answer the question of why long-term decline continues unnoticed or unchecked and, for some, this is just the natural order of things. Unless you are talking about earthquakes, the moon's gravitational impact on the earth or eclipses of the sun, there is nothing natural in football. Our predicament is manmade and can only be changed by deliberate intervention. But decline also creates the conditions in which self-interest, or special interests, can establish greater authority, influence, and power, especially when the game is not anchored to a long-term plan, vision, and ambition. Lacking any real democracy or any effective outside involvement in governance, the future of the game is largely in the hands of the few to the real exclusion of the many and possibly the wider common good of the game. The game is splintered, fractured, and fragmented. There is no common purpose and what we have arrived at is a group of competing interests, issues and institutions that will remain rooted in the day-to-day struggles, the short term, and the battle over finance. This is the most important reason why the game, in its current form, is destined to decline and disappoint, and continue to diminish itself in the eyes of the wider Scottish public and government. No one doubts the complex nature of the game and the difficult challenges facing the SFA and the SPFL, but the institutions must recognise that there are a diverse range of competing interests and priorities, some of which will lose out, unless there is a radical shake up and rebalancing of how football in Scotland is run.

There is a different and better future for Scottish football. But what does success look like? In the US, legendary basketball coach, John Wooden, says it's a matter of satisfaction: 'Success is peace of mind, which is a direct result of self-satisfaction in knowing you did your best to become the best you are capable of becoming.' Churchill thought success is being relentless. Thomas Edison said, 'Success is one per cent inspiration and 99 per cent perspiration.' Success can be elusive. It is often hard to define, difficult to measure and it requires collective intent and a commitment from all those involved. Winning is part of success. But for Scots, the most important single issue is regularly qualifying for international tournaments that will, in turn, keep citizen and country engaged and supportive of Scottish football. For Scotland, I would argue that this remains the most powerful measure of success. This is also our biggest failure over the last 20 years. Serious questions must be asked as to where this priority of the people fits into the priorities of those who run the game. Regardless of the difficulty of defining success, we are on safer ground when we assert that our national game is underachieving and underperforming relative to both our spectacular history, our achievements in the 60s, 70s, 80s and early 90s, and the undoubted talent that still exists in every part of Scotland.

Sometimes, I wonder if my obsession with the game feeds off itself and takes me into a world only populated with other obsessives who are nostalgic, sentimental and possibly delusional. As a baby boomer – do I have too much of the San Francisco flower power gene of the 1960s?

Or was I just fortunate at the age of 12 to watch Real Madrid beat Eintracht Frankfurt, 7-3 at Hampden park in the European Cup final?

Or is it the fact that my old club East Fife, the only second division club to win the Scottish cup in 1937/8, played in front of 400,000 fans in the cup run that year?

Or did I only dream about Archie Gemmill scoring one of the greatest goals ever, beating Holland, 3-2 in the 1978 World cup?

Or have I ever gotten over watching Scotland beat World Cup winners, England in 1967, when Jim Baxter played 'keepie uppie' and tormented the life out of the weary English players?

Or do I still enjoy the fact that Celtic were the first British team to win the European cup with their 2-1 victory in Lisbon in 1967?

Have we obsessives become untethered from reality? Have memories and delusions come back to distort reality and give me an over optimistic view of the beautiful game? Are we hanging on to a world, real or imaginary, where football dominated our lives to such an extent, that it 'was more than a game', indeed 'more important than life itself'? Has my natural childhood football environment, and each of its overlapping parts – cultural, religious, identity, class, political, intellectual, psychological, sociological, philosophical, and sadly tribal – created the conditions for distorted and highly selective lapses of memory and reality?

I don't think so.

Although I will own up to some of this, what is remarkable is the fact that we, as a football loving nation, have retained an infinite capacity for emotion, pride, and passion regardless of the state of the game. Hope springs eternal. The gap between our expectations and achievements, especially at international level, never narrows. At club level, a few compete for trophies, whilst many clubs only compete to survive; all of this supported by loyal, devoted and long-suffering fans.

Setting aside for a minute the obsessives, there is a grudging acknowledgement that Scottish football is very special, has a remarkable history, a record of success and achievement, still touches hearts and minds, and remains a vital part of the life, soul and spirit of our country; however frustrating, disappointing and dispiriting this can be at times.

But how long can this last? Regardless of where we are on the spectrum of this love-hate relationship, the main priority for all of us is to wake up to the fact that the game has lost its way and that there is an urgency in finding a way back: but a way back to what?

I own up to being an obsessive. But I am also, after a long relationship with the game, as a player, politician and a reviewer of the game for the SFA in 2010, a person with the best interests of a new and confident Scotland close to my heart, a passionate pragmatist and a critical friend of Scottish football. Nor am I blinkered to the very real problems, pressures and challenges facing the game. This book has not been written by a neutral or dispassionate observer of the game.

The game must do more for itself. A closed, exclusive, defensive and insecure game cannot make a giant leap forward. The timeless emotions of pride, passion and patriotism as well as excitement, drama and indeed tragedy, requires our search for success to rise above vested interests, limited horizons and diminishing expectations, which are now sadly an integral feature of our national psyche. The law of diminishing expectations is corrosive and eventually self-defeating.

The book is necessarily hard hitting, but based on a tough yet fair analysis. Other footballing nations are moving quickly. We are not. Twenty years on from qualifying for either the World Cup or the European Championships, Scottish football must accept it is running out of time and excuses. We have to ease up on blaming personalities, and playing a blame game that moves quickly and provides short-term relief and respite, but for most of the time, delivers little substance. Chairmen, managers, chief executives and performance directors come and go, but in Scotland, the structural, institutional and cultural problems remain. Instead we must accept that deep-seated issues lie at the heart of our problems and when linked to a rapidly changing nation, society and lifestyles, the challenge becomes formidable, and possibly overwhelming. But for some, the 'too difficult' response becomes a powerful excuse for inactivity and a further step to decline.

This is difficult territory, at the start of the 21st century, in which to engineer a renaissance of Scottish football when much of its spiritual and cultural foundations were set down in the first half of the last century. To have the remotest chance of this happening, we must climb above the toxic, cynical, hostile and pessimistic atmosphere that is stifling progress and accept instead a more collective responsibility for the state of Scottish football and its future.

Signals and Noise

Similar to politics, there is always a great deal of 'noise' surrounding the game: acres and acres of newsprint, loads of electronic chatter and abuse, highly informed comment and positive ideas from specialist journalists and pundits and much more informed contributions from fan organisations. There is no shortage of coverage. In this electronic age, there is also a great deal of highly destructive and personally abusive material that does the game a great disservice. This often impacts on the world outside football and, like some of the television coverage, travels abroad. We should be wise to the fact that 'local' now means 'global'. Ignoring the dark and destructive parts of the debate, the game – recognised as the SPFL and SFA – do not appear to be listening or willing to take on board some of the positive ideas, which could help reform the game. There is a wealth of football knowledge outside the game that should be listened to.

Looking forward there are three very simple scenarios for the future of the game.

The **'muddling along scenario'** is easy. Reflecting the weariness of the current debate, this view rejects any overly optimistic vision and adopts the culture of contentment. People like me are asked to abandon what some perceive as the sentiment, nostalgia and memories of a bygone era and argue instead that we should be realistic and live in the real world. Scottish football through this prism, is seen as living within a limited or narrow ambition, shackled by the pressures of finance and unconcerned about the bigger picture. This vision of the future is no longer framed around the remarkable achievements of our past and the possibilities and potential that might lie ahead. The game remains shackled to pessimism and the corroding cynicism that, for far too long, has been a constant feature of the game.

Another scenario, **'club game wins over country'**, suggests that we carry on as we are but accepts that the beautiful game has a mixed future, and limited significance for country and our national side. Achievements will be found around successful club football for the few, disappointment and struggle for the many, and the success of the national side becomes less and less significant, or important. Project Brave, a key part of our youth strategy, is already in danger of becoming a causality of this scenario as the ambition, finance, priorities and resources are favouring the few, at the expense of the many and abandoning a nationwide nurturing of talent. The lack of an effective debate within the game, the lack of democracy, the absence of transparency, an unequal distribution of power and finance and a weak membership structure are all helping to undermine the national game.

The weakening of the SFA – custodian of the national game – is a crucial factor in this scenario. Powerful interests hold sway and the prospects for radical change are much more limited than they have been previously. The common good of football is at risk if there is a consolidation of this strategy to strengthen the finances and opportunities of the few, at the expense of the national game, youth development and our chances of international success.

I believe the 'muddling along' scenario and the 'club game wins over country' scenario are not in the best interests of Scottish football, hold little prospect for achieving radical reforms and pay scant regard to the spirit, success, history and potential of the game. They also pose a threat to a Scottish talent-based revival and will hold back programmes urgently needed to bring coherence, purpose and modernity to the game. The **'optimistic club and country approach'** is rooted in building a better future for the game that, without apology, is based on the spirit of the famous quote of Bill Shankly:

> Some people believe football is a matter of life and death. I am very disappointed with that attitude. I can assure you it is much more important than that.

The Football Aspiration Gap

Optimism, self-belief, ambition and vision are the foundations for a better future for Scottish football. And it all revolves around what I would describe as the 'Football Aspiration Gap'. Carrying on as we are may be 'okay', but will do nothing to bridge the football aspiration gap. On the one hand, there is our enlightened past, our football history, our human resource or football capital, our, in my view, world-class assets and our passion and aspirations. On the other, our current and more limited achievements and underperformance, our undistinguished international performance relative to World and European indicators and our hesitant, narrow, and uncertain attitude. Reinforcing this limited worldview is a set of seemingly intractable, complex and enduring problems, not helped by a growing and profound pessimism of fans, and public generally, about the state of the game. There is also the game's uneasy relationship with new ideas, new thinking, and the idea of change itself. This is a national dilemma.

Alex Ferguson; great Scot, brilliant manager and a real patriot. The giants of football were good at their trade but unlike many modern managers and administrators, they were also very connected to the wider Scotland and seemed enthusiastic about their patriotism. Club and country were indivisible. This matters. The problems of Scottish football cannot be separated from the wider issues of modern society and the latent potential that exists for a bigger success story for the country. There is an illuminating example of what is needed.

Ryder Cup

Golf's Ryder Cup was last held in Scotland at Muirfield in 1973 and I felt that after 30 years, it should return. In this of all sports, our credentials go before us; the home of golf with some of the most famous, challenging and beautiful courses in the world, was more than qualified to put in a world-class bid. I saw the significance of staging major sporting and cultural events as matters of national prestige, pride, and prosperity. The Ryder Cup satisfied all requirements. We decided to support a bid for the 2008 Ryder Cup and in stepped patriot, Ferguson. The final presentation of what Scotland had to offer was made at a dinner at Stirling Castle. We made sure it was a wonderful evening of which Scotland could be immensely proud. It brought together some of the best golf courses in the world with the best support services and a unique video presentation, hosted by sports presenter Dougie Donnelly. It included national heroes, Colin Montgomerie, Jackie Stewart, Sean Connery and Sam Torrance, the victorious Ryder Cup captain. But we needed more icing on the cake. At the last minute, I phoned Sir Alex at old Trafford and asked him if he would come to Stirling and help promote his country. Without hesitation, he said he would be absolutely delighted to be 'on the team'. Football was bigger than Ferguson, Shankly, Stein and Busby but for them Scotland was bigger than the game. Scotland was a team game. I am not sure Scottish football today thinks or acts like this and it too often seems remote from national aspirations, instead preoccupied with the immediacy of its own problems. The outcome was positive. Despite the political skulduggery of the Ryder Cup Committee, we forced them, for the first time in their history, to decide on the venue for two events, one in Wales in 2009 and the other in Scotland in 2013.

The Euros

To me, as First Minister, it seemed a logical step after backing the highly successful return of golf's Ryder Cup to Scotland, that we should bid for another great sporting event in football's European Championship. Apart from my passion for the game, it seemed a fitting recognition for the country that had given so much to the game and whose supporters were acclaimed as the best in the world; long suffering but brilliant. I was initially dismayed and surprised by the lack of interest and enthusiasm from a wide cross-section of Scottish life, including the Scottish Football Association. Once again, lack of ambition and the fear of failure were constant companions in Scottish attitude and football was no exception. Nearly 20 years on, we still seem to have this millstone around our necks. We were well provided with stadia and I believed we could have met the FIFA and UEFA requirement for six to eight world-class grounds. We would have Hampden, Murrayfield, Parkhead, Ibrox, Pittodrie in Aberdeen, the two main clubs in Edinburgh and Dundee, and possibly Rugby Park in Kilmarnock. Doubters suggested that a number of these stadia would need improvement but that was by no means insurmountable. When the Dutch and Belgians combined to present the finals in 2000, they put up temporary seating that met all the standards and was later removed. We could certainly do better than that. The necessary ground improvements might have cost £70 million, not necessarily from public funds but from mixed public-private finance and would have created first-class facilities for community use. The result would have been hundreds of millions of pounds in income, and again, an incalculable boost for Scotland's international image.

As First Minster, in 2001 I led the bid for the European Championships to be played in Scotland in 2008. It was always a long shot but I had to persuade and cajole the Scottish Football Association to bid. We were not successful but my instincts were to be ambitious, be confident and put Scotland on the world football stage. Interestingly, I took questions on a local radio station and an older man rang in to say I shouldn't have made the effort. When I asked him why he had this view, he said, 'Because we might lose...' I thought this was very Scottish and only made me more determined to put Scotland, in a football sense, first. The 'tall poppy syndrome', 'know your place' and I 'kent your faither' attitudes have always irritated and challenged me. We are a great deal better than we think at times.

My football aspiration gap is defined as the 'future we aspire to and the one we will create if we only rely on current modes of thought and behaviour'. This concept is borrowed from work done by the Royal Society of Arts (RSA) in London. We accept that in certain specific areas of national life, such as medicine, biosciences, education, technology, renewables and financial services, Scotland is a world-class performer. We will address the issue of achieving that status in Scotland as a modern football nation reflecting a confidence and self-belief (national football self-worth), as well as being perceived internationally as having a brand which others recognise and respect (global worth), in the coming chapters. The work of the RSA represents a new way of looking at the complex reality of football and poses the fundamental question, 'What do we need to do to create the football future we want?'

Bridging the aspiration gap in Scottish football encourages the prospect of helping to understand better: what we need to do to anticipate and cope with change; what the results of change would be; and, in the process, outline what Scottish football would be like in the future and what specific benefits would be achieved, and for whom.

We should not underestimate the challenge of change. In a complex football world, change is hard, demanding, threatening and it challenges our innate conservatism. Change requires inspiration, innovation, and enthusiasm. It calls for dramatic timescales and deadlines, especially in a climate of intense and intensifying competition; our club and national opponents, abroad and in the UK, are not standing still, this is a continuing catch up. Change needs leadership, focus and discipline but also needs self-belief, self-confidence and self-esteem. Change in the new football world order needs a new world-view and a new sense of purpose and role for Scottish football. Change is difficult to start and difficult to manage. But Willie Malley, Bill Struth, Jock Stein, Alex Ferguson, Bill Shankly and Matt Busby managed change and won success.

It is much easier to be complacent and comfortable. Some would argue that we are getting by, but for how much longer? It is one thing to believe and aspire to a new vision of Scottish football, but it is much more difficult to escape from current modes of thought and behaviour, and deliver. For change to happen, a certain number of important factors must be in place and all of the evidence from other successful changes in sport suggest that this 'transformational mix' or 'aspirational elixir' doesn't just happen but has to be carefully created. How was Scotland's current football outlook shaped over nearly 150 years? How well placed is football to respond to these new realities? Are there qualities that separate us apart from other nations? Our positive traits are often understated and undersold as we let ill-informed criticism and negative sentiment overwhelm us, dominating our national psyche and undermining our national mood and morale. What will it take to bridge this aspirational football gap in Scotland, acknowledging that we are talking about an unforgiving and restless society, and a complex football culture?

There are significant forces at work, creating stresses and a crisis of complexity as society issues become more intricate with the rate of change truly breath taking, and institutions become more and more handicapped by the slow pace at which they can evolve and adapt. In Scottish football, one of the big issues is raising the game of those in charge of governance. Traditional thinking and current institutional behaviour must change. This is the central idea at the heart of transforming Scottish football. If we are to achieve a world-class standard of club and international football, then we must deliver solutions to urgent issues, faster and more effectively.

Scottish football has to be rebuilt on strong and solid pillars. The proposed pillars of the new structure are:

- A sustainable, attractive, and successful club game where incentive, ideas and inspiration are available to radically improve and maintain the clubs in the Premiere League. Not only to drastically improve the offer to fans on the pitch but to transform the conditions, the environment and facilities and to encourage a younger and more diversified fan and supporter base. European football is the key to club success and in addition to the cumulative benefits of coefficients and financial rewards, fans deserve to see the best clubs in Europe. They excite and enthuse, and help keep our ambitions firmly rooted at the highest level. Celtic, Rangers and Aberdeen swept away all before them to become European Champions.

- For aspiring clubs in the Championship who are seeking success in the title race, the Scottish Cup and League Cup, more recognition and priority are long overdue. The distribution of power and finance in Scottish football favours the Premier League. A powerful Championship is an effective bridge between the lower Scottish leagues and the Premier league. The football authorities could, and should, be doing more to improve the quality of at this level.

- For the part-time/part-professional leagues, one and two, there are different challenges and opportunities to deal with. There will always be a role for the smaller clubs in cup competitions where a favourable draw could provide a shock result, excitement for the fans, moments of glory for club and community, and, in certain cases, a huge financial bonus. But at this level, as well as keeping a strong involvement with the traditional game, new opportunities need to be grasped. Most of the clubs are involved in community development. In the future, this could be developed further especially in the fields of sport, health, fitness, well-being and confidence building amongst children, young people, and adults. In addition, our comprehensive grass roots football network provides local authorities and government with unparalleled coverage and a proven track-record of community commitment.

- The national game outside the formal league structure is a remarkable asset for football and the country, and is a replenishing source of talent. In our drive to transform our elite youth development through club and regional academies, the massive number of other organisations shouldn't be overlooked. They also provide the facilities to grow the numbers of people playing the game – with all the associated health benefits – which must now be around 500,000 people in Scotland.

- The international game and the national team are at most risk as we continue to fail to qualify for the final stages of the World Cup and European Championships. Twenty years is a long time and is especially significant relative to our remarkable run of success in the 20 years prior to 1998, the quality of Scottish talent that this country has produced, and clearly with the same source of DNA, could produce in the future. How did we let this slip away? This is the overarching challenge and the biggest and most pressing problem facing Scottish football. This seems to be no longer the priority it once was, if results are anything to go by.

- An integral part of our failure to win success at the national level is our poor record of identifying elite youth talent, nurturing those golden qualities, and eventually ensuring they are given opportunities to display their skills for club and country. This is now a crisis. Amidst the massive changes in every aspect of our lives over the last 30 years, we collectively, have comprehensively failed to understand what was happening. We left it to a few of our clubs to serve the national interest. They didn't. We left it to the clubs to be discerning and careful with the number and quality of the foreign players they were signing. They didn't. We left it to all the clubs to think young and give new talent an opportunity to shine. They didn't. Scotland's elite talent, its long-suffering national fans and the soul of the nation need a new deal. Clubs need to survive in difficult financial times and tough choices must be made, so we need to reconsider certain trends. We are wasting the football wealth of a nation.

CHAPTER THREE

Deep Roots in Rich Soil

OUTSIDERS SAW METHIL IN the '40s and '50s as a grim, grimy and unattractive place, but those of us who were born and brought up there are proud of it. When I was born there in 1948, at 50 Morar Street, it seemed as if the town was stuck in the previous century. Homebirths were still common and, true to Scottish working-class tradition, I spent my first night in a drawer as a makeshift crib because my parents had not been able to buy a cot or pram. The young couple starting their own family had moved in with my grandmother's family, and at any time there were at least ten people living in a four-roomed house.

A once-prosperous coal-loading port on the Firth of Forth, Methil was dominated by the local pits and bings: a town of Victorian slums and miners' rows with seemingly endless trains of coal wagons, running night and day down to the harbour and returning empty. In winter it was bleak, and in summer, we played along the beaches and the tidemark was drawn in coal dust. The Third Statistical Account of Scotland in 1951 said Methil was 'an overgrown mining village, unbalanced and with no "West End"'. A century before, it had been described as 'one of the most perfect pictures of decay to be met anywhere in Scotland'. Following the heyday of the coal trade in the early twentieth century, the decline began again. This was accelerated in the '50s and '60s with the closure of coalfields across the region, and locally, that of Wellesley Colliery and the showpiece Michael Colliery, after a disastrous fire which killed nine men. Miners and dockworkers were laid off, the pitheads and harbour were dismantled and the last working pit in the area, Lochhead Colliery at the well-named Coaltown of Wemyss, closed in 1970. The closure of the Frances and Seafield collieries in the '80s and '90s would seal the fate of coalmining in Fife. Later, as Fife council leader, I was proud to play a part in the rejuvenation and restoration of my hometown.

Despite the harshness and deterioration, it was, and still is, a warm, welcoming and special place to me. I grew up there surrounded by hardworking, tolerant and community-minded people. I played in safety, developed at my own pace and was given every chance to better myself – a chance I almost threw away. I had the classic Scottish coalfield upbringing; the son and grandson of miners, living in a street of mine workers. Fife was built on coal and from the Industrial Revolution until the 1960s, coal was king. When I was born, there were 50 pits and 50,000 mineworkers in the county. These days are now gone.

My grandfather, Henry Cunningham Baird, was born in 1888 and died in 1965. I got my love of football from him. He played for East Fife between 1908 and 1913, when thousands of men left – some never to return – to fight in the First World War.

At the end of the war he returned home traumatised, now known as Post Traumatic Stress Syndrome and took a while to recover before returning to the mine. He had problems with alcohol but then became an Evangelical Christian, joining the Plymouth Brethern. Being from Methil, he was of course a socialist.

He worked in the mines with the privately owned Wemyss Coal Company. It was hard listening to his stories about life in the pits and the hardship of digging coal in dangerous conditions: the solidarity in mining communities was a product of adversity, hardship and common purpose.

He was a remarkable man, spiritual and political, and I was privileged to have him as a grandfather. He was also a tireless activist and practiced what he preached. Working in the soup kitchens during the 1926 Miners' strike, he was dedicated to what we would now recognise as progressive thinking. It didn't seem so progressive on Sundays when I had to hide my football kit and sneak out to play without receiving a few verses on the sanctity of the Sabbath. Even more remarkable was his passion for the beautiful game. Much later and after he died, I found some fascinating photographs and text from the local newspapers. I had a few pictures of him with his East Fife strip but then I found two other pictures, which illustrated to me, a really vibrant and innovative period football that was going through in the early 1900s. One showed him with five of his mates standing beside a large basket with the name, 'Methil Thursday F.C.' on it. The other was when he played in 1908 for a team called, 'Methil Navahoe Juveniles'. The caption read, not surprisingly, 'Here come the Indians'.

In the early history of similar communities throughout Scotland, the game was flourishing and would eventually produce future giants of the game like Jock Stein, Alex Ferguson, Matt Busby, and Bill Shankly. However, two World wars were to take their toll on my grandfather's generation.

Thousands of young Scots never came home and would never play again for the thousands of teams that they had helped form and which contributed, in large measure, to building a solid foundation for the game, and its success, in the immediate post war period.

The early history of the game brought out the best in working people; that sense of local identity and place, the generation of local heroes and a focus for their pride and passion which established so many of these incredible loyalties that we can now see today in every part of Scotland. Being part, of all of this, even in a very modest way, is a privilege. These same communities experienced mining disasters and it is easy to see why class and solidarity became so important in shaping lives. Many local communities, and their clubs, have experienced enormous changes over the years but our modern game must be sure to respect their achievements. Football was a way of life, and for some in the modern era, it remains so. Football's role in the history of the Scotland should never be overlooked or underestimated, but always seen as a reminder of what was and still could be: our football lineage, our DNA, our remarkable contribution to social history, our successes and achievements, our contribution to football's greatest moments. Looking ahead, it is our legacy and we must build on it.

When my father left school at 14 and went down the pit, it was his choice – but at the time he had no real option because he knew the family needed the reasonable money that he could earn. Now, when we think of a boy of 14 going underground, we can see it was child labour and the worst form of exploitation. He was underground for 30 years and when he came up for the last time at the age of 44, he was on a stretcher with his legs shattered.

Long before that happened, my father declared that none of his sons would go down the mines. When I finally went down the Frances Colliery on an official visit as a councillor, I saw why. Even in what was supposed to be a 'modern' mine, I could not understand how people could work in such hellish conditions, like human moles amid darkness, dirt and danger, crawling about in narrow seams, doing gruelling physical work and literally dragging the coal out by brute force. When they went down for their shift, they knew their lives were in danger, yet they accepted that as the everyday risk. These conditions also produced some of Scotland's finest players and managers.

When I was two or three, my mother and father moved to Institution Row, a line of miners' cottages with outside toilets, known locally as 'Irish raw'. In 1952, we moved to a new housing estate for mineworkers, which were being grafted on to the old village of Kennoway.

Until I was 15 when I left school and signed for Leeds United FC, all I did was play football. I wanted nothing to do with education. When I was 12, my record for 'keepie uppies' was 1,760. It took me 20 minutes and, because I stood on my left foot throughout, I had it in plaster because of the strain. (My record with the much more difficult tennis ball, by the way, was 400.) So that was the sum total of my achievement by the age of 15, a pretty pointless 'keepie uppie' record.

While still attending school, I experienced the hardest work I have ever done in my life – driven by my love of football – because I desperately wanted a Real Madrid strip. (I could never recite much Burns or Shakespeare but I could (and still can) recite the Real line-up of the day: Dominguez, Marquitos, Pachin, Vidal, Santamaria, Zarraga, Canario, del Sol, Di Stefano, Puskas, Gento). In those days, older schoolchildren were released from school to help with the potato harvest. My mother, who was at the time 'tattie-howking', said if I went for a day I would earn enough for a Real strip. It was back-breaking work and the 14s 11½d for that one day was the hardest-earned money I ever made.

It was no surprise that when I left Buckhaven High School in 1963 I received a report card that summed up my life to that point and became a wake-up call for me to change my attitude. The rector's parting comment was: 'I am glad the boy is a good footballer, because he has no future in education.'

One of the main criticisms of my young self is that I didn't do enough reading. My father was an avid reader and a member of a book club, but I chose not to read the books young people should read and was not exposed to great literature, music and art. In the community where I grew up, these were not regarded as important. They were wasted years and for the rest of my life I have been trying to fill that cultural black hole. That is why I have advocated free music tuition in every Scottish school, maximum access to the arts and encouraged children to read.

I missed out on an amazing amount of learning and education and it was largely through my own choice. My report cards were a bigger disappointment to my parents than to me because I regarded school as a necessary evil, and during school holidays and at weekends played football all day long. I did nothing academically and was getting 20% for French and 18% for maths, but I was athletics and tennis champion and playing representative football, captaining Fife County. It was a football-daft schoolboy's dream come true when I was invited to Elland Road, Leeds United's ground, for a trial and was signed by the great Don Revie. But I was home and back at school eight weeks later.

My brief Leeds adventure began one Saturday. I was captain of Fife Schools in a game against Dundee Schools. We won 5-2 and I scored a hat trick. Unknown to me, the Leeds United scout was on the touchline and on the following Sunday morning on my way, as ever, to play football, an old man in a long coat and white cap stopped me and said he was looking for 'the boy McLeish'. Mystified, I told him that was me, and he said, 'I'll have to speak to your mum and dad.'

As a boy from a Scots working-class background, that was the start of my real education. Leeds United looked after boys from very different backgrounds and they taught me things I would not have otherwise learned. They took us to a top-class hotel for the first time and showed us which cutlery to use. It was training for life, not just football, so that we would not embarrass ourselves, or the club.

I just couldn't get used to being away from home, however, which is hardly surprising at that age. Although some other talented youngsters I shared digs with went on to international stardom and are still idolised. They included Eddie Gray, who was destined to be one of Scotland's great players, as well as Peter Lorimer, and Jackie Charlton who was in the third team. For me, it was a privilege to clean the boots of the great Celtic and Scotland player, Bobby Collins.

Back home, I signed for the local club, East Fife, when I was 16 – the youngest player ever to play for them – and my first game was in March 1964 against Queen's Park at Hampden. There were only 900 people in the stadium, which could hold 130,000 at that time, but it was still an enormous thrill to walk through the dressing rooms and out onto that historic pitch. When I was 18, I was picked for a trial for Scotland against a select side at Motherwell. We lost 5-1, but the *Daily Record* report of the game said, 'Only one young Scot impressed – Henry McLeish of East Fife, who scored a cracking opening goal.'

As a footballer at that time, you became a bit of a local hero. You might not have made great academic achievements, but you were still highly regarded in your community. It was a big thing for my classmates when the team bus would come up to the school gates to pick me up before an away game. I was then selected for the Scotland team for the Youth World Cup, hosted by Yugoslavia in Pristina, the now infamous capital of Kosovo. We drew all three of our games. However, my abiding memory of the game against Holland was that the organisers didn't have the Scottish national anthem. At that time, it was 'Scotland the Brave'. My heart was beating proudly as I lined up, waiting for the national anthem to be played. But instead of the anthem, they played 'Island of Dreams' by The Springfields: you can understand why I have remained close to this tune.

We drew with Holland 1-1, and true to the performances of our senior counterparts at that time, 1966, we didn't progress from the group stages. Pristina where we were based is now part of the newly created and contested country of Kosovo, and its capital. At that time, it was part of the Communist country of Yugoslavia, where President Tito ruled, with his photograph behind every bar and in every restaurant. Being a Dictatorship, there was certainly never any trouble on the streets, but neither was there much food on the table. Our hotel was built in an area of terrible poverty, with children scavenging for food.

I have always been infuriated when I have had lectures from so-called 'nationalists' who doubt the patriotism of other Scots, their support for their county and their flag. I never need reminding about what it means to be a Scot. I have a youth international cap; I have worn the blue jersey and the blazer with the Scottish badge; I have represented Scotland in my country's greatest sport. I have always been more nationalist-minded (with a small 'n') than some of my Labour colleagues. It may have been football, my upbringing or my background that made me raise issues of national identity. I would ask, 'Why shouldn't the Labour Party be identifiably the party of Scotland?' To other Scottish Labour colleagues, it had to be an identifiably United Kingdom party.

I still believe that sport at the highest level is an asset for any nation. Scotland has produced world-class sportsmen and women, so being a small nation is not a real excuse for failing to strive for the highest level of attainment. That is why sport was high on my political agenda; not just because of the benefits of participating in sport, but also for the prestige that comes with staging events like the European football championship and the Ryder Cup.

Sport is a populist way of getting people to feel better about their own country. It does not mean you are a narrow nationalist. It does not mean you take a parish-pump view. It does not mean you then go on from football to blame the English for everything in life. It does mean that you promote the best of your country and are ambitious for your country; a small nation on the periphery of Europe to achieve a leading place in the world. As I was to later discover, that kind of ambition for Scotland is singularly lacking in many of our politicians.

Football taught me the importance of self-worth and I still believe it is an important lesson for Scotland in the wider world. Even though we have world-class people and world-class resources, we are being held back by a lack of confidence in our own abilities.

But there was another, less glamorous, facet to football. Playing with East Fife and junior clubs like Glenrothes Juniors and St Andrews United, I visited every part of Scotland and played on nearly every club pitch in the country – in working-class areas, in towns and cities, and in mining and fishing communities. Football brought me closer to Scottish life and culture.

The other thing football gave me from my early years and which lasted throughout my political life, was a competitive urge. I used to berate people who asked, when my team had lost, 'Did you enjoy the game?' Even as a lad, any enjoyment I got depended on the result. I liked playing, but I loved winning and I would reply, 'We were beaten. How could I enjoy that?' I never believed in that high-minded public school sentiment: 'It isn't the winning that matters, but the taking part.' From what I seen of public schoolboys, especially in politics, they are very bad losers. Like them, I was with the American coach who declared: 'Winning isn't everything. It's the only thing.'

I was in midfield, and later left-back, at a time when football was a tough business, but not as dirty as the modern professional game has become. When I see players on mega-salaries bringing the game into disrepute – spitting, jersey pulling, diving, shielding the ball and getting opponents sent off – I do not recognise it as the same game. I played at a ferociously competitive level and am afraid I have to agree with the club historian who described me as an 'uncompromising' tackler. Challenges were bone jarring and a 50-50 ball usually meant two hospital cases. Even in a friendly match with workmates, I went in so hard that I broke my leg. When I was taken into the Kirkcaldy Hospital, I was wheeled through to my father who was still a patient there, recovering from his horrendous leg injuries. It made my injury seem so trivial.

A teammate summed me up to a political profile writer: 'He took no prisoners, but perhaps was not the silkiest of footballers.' The same writer added, 'His managers, meanwhile, would complain that he too often came out of position' – something my MSP colleagues have noted that I continued to do. If my football and political careers have to be compared, I prefer the assessment of family friend and lifelong East Fife supporter, Lord Harry Ewing. He remembered me as 'a superb anticipator of opposition attacks'.

Returning to School

On my return from Leeds, I packed into three years at school, all that I had missed in the previous years of squandered opportunity. I took my second chance and left with three Highers and ten O-levels. I make no recriminations and I am not bitter, but I was only too aware of the gaps in my education. It is something I nearly missed out on completely because I was a stubborn boy who was obsessed by football.

The lesson I learned, and which I have tried to put into effect throughout my political career, is that most youngsters have something to offer, but at a moment in time are either not interested, or developed enough to exploit it. I was lucky to have the opportunity later to show my potential that could be developed. My political purpose has always been to make sure every child does not make the mistakes I did – and, if they do, to ensure they have a second chance, or as many chances as they need in life.

I also believe that Scottish education often fails to make our young people confident or give them a sense of their own worth. I have always tried to appear assured, but I was never that confident anywhere other than on the football field. When Scottish boys and girls leave school they are expected to 'know their place', which leads to pigeonholing and the stifling of both personal initiative and the enterprise our country needs so badly. They should leave school with a healthy regard for their own qualities and knowledge of how they can improve themselves. Above all, they should have been taught that 'their place' is whatever they want to make it.

CHAPTER FOUR

Anatomy of the Game

When I left Buckhaven High School, for the first time in 1963, I received a report card, which summed up the importance of football in my life. The rector's parting comment was: 'I am glad the boy is a good footballer, because he has no future in education.'

IT HAS BEEN SAID that for many Scots, football is akin to a religion, with its fervour and (sometimes misplaced) faith. So much of Scottish life and our national sense of identity have been wrapped up in the game. For myself, a constellation of factors and events aligned to shape and mould a football-mad, working-class kid who has retained, to this day, a life-long passion for the game; perhaps a combined obsession with football and politics, both rooted in community.

Football has played an important part in my personal story. For me it is about a sense of place, culture, identity, class, community, solidarity and purpose. My love for the game has been that of millions of typical Scots through the years but, more than that, I owe a debt to football for lifting me out of the ordinary and it is that debt I now hope to repay. I confess that I write – first, foremost and always – as a football fan. I have additional insights as a former professional player, as a politician and someone with experience of public life. However, the best fans are those who are realistic and are prepared to bring common sense to bear, along with the passion and commitment. We can look back fondly on the days when the influences of working-class life, social togetherness and national pride combined in Scotland to create a remarkable set of circumstance in which Scottish football flourished, post-war and up until the 1980's.

However, now is a time to be realistic and admit that Scottish Football is in what can appear to be an endless and relentless cycle of declining expectations, under-achievement and under-performance on the field, especially at international level – not to mention a loss of purpose and authority in its administration.

The 'Auld Enemy' Triumphs

This Scottish decline is felt most keenly when compared to the 2018 World Cup, achievements which have given England a new sense of national identity and togetherness. For good or ill, Scottish football will always be judged – and too often found wanting – in the light of the contrasting fortunes of our cross-border neighbours.

English football achieves. But in Scotland, the national game is challenged by history, institutional inertia and seems permanently insecure about its future. Our game is fragmented and lacks direction and purpose. There seems to be no big ambition, no sense of sustained anger or urgency about the fact that a once spectacularly successful footballing nation needn't be in this precarious and uninspiring place.

Few people writing a book on the future of Scottish football have had the privilege of writing a few paragraphs over a cup of coffee on the sun-drenched battlefield at Culloden Moor. Visiting Inverness to deliver a talk on Brexit, this is always a good stopover to charge batteries, not in any nostalgic nationalist way but merely to enjoy a great historic place and to reflect in what is a strangely peaceful part of Scotland.

Culloden was the last battle ever fought on British soil, in 1746. The Jacobites were routed and destroyed by the Hanoverians in the same time it takes to play the first half of a Scottish Premiere League game. For some strange reason, my mind drifted to the fixture between Scotland and England, which was played annually between 1872 and 1983. In the early days of the game, after the SFA was created in 1873, the Scotland vs. England match made a great deal of sense. These were the first two countries to form associations. Some of the games were spectacular battles, clashes of historic proportions, providing some magnificent football and some of the highest attendances ever seen in world football.

For some extremists, it was historic enmity and so much emotional capital has been invested in our games with England. This is not to say these historic clashes, with crowds we can now only dream about, did not matter. But the true importance to Scottish football was past its sell-by date.

In my view, the Home Championship and the Scotland-England fixture had become a major distraction for a country that needed to invest more in European and International football, direct the patriotism and nationalism of Scotland to bigger ambitions and call time on a game in which Scots had invested too much emotional capital. We had distorted our football values by attaching too much importance and significance to defeating the auld enemy. It made sense for this fixture to be abandoned in 1983.

The ultimate distortion was in 1950, when the winners and runners-up in the Home Championship had automatic entry to the final stages of the World Cup. England won that year, but rather than go to the World Cup as runners up, Scotland declined the opportunity to participate. This decision did not go down well in Scotland. We had to wait until 1954 to play in the first International tournament post-1945 then we also qualified for the 1958 World Cup, but then had to wait another 16 years, until 1974, to qualify again.

Our pre-occupation with beating England, and for too many bigots, hating England, may have been at the expense of investing more emotional capital and national fervour in other directions. Obviously, it was a great event with the spectacle of two of the oldest football nations colliding, but at what cost? Our football, like our politics, has too often seen England as an historical focus for our weaknesses and opprobrium, not our strengths and ambition.

The wisdom of such a long running fixture is a debating point. There is no doubt that in the mind-set of many Scots and football supporters, successive games against England have been used as a rerun of history where broader themes of country, pride, passion, grudge and grievance have engulfed the beautiful game. Settling old scores and rerunning old battles are less important than winning success in this new global game.

England reached new heights in the 2018 World Cup in Russia, but Scotland was not there. Our, fans, players and people, had to watch on television. And yet another small country, Iceland, was also there. Iceland? This is embarrassing. For 20 years and five World Cups we have failed to qualify. For 22 years and five European Championships we have failed to qualify. In two years, Iceland has been in France and Russia. We are fading fast from the minds of the international footballing community. This is not acceptable, but neither is it inevitable or an act of God. This crisis is homegrown.

The founding fathers of our great game must be turning in their graves as we squander the legacy of the early years and replace the Golden Age of Scottish football, the 60s to 90s, with decline, non-achievement, less ambition for our national team and a failure to take responsibility for what we are doing. Everything happens for a reason. We have no excuses left to spin. We need to accept that we are not good enough and start to rebuild.

We do live in a different Scotland and perhaps the advent of devolution and the growth of nationalism have shifted some of our energy, enthusiasm, and passion for the game, away from football and on to politics. Maybe we have bought into the idea that the present state of the game is all we can expect. Maybe one of the most successful footballing nations has run out of the self-belief that created so many legends and inspiring memories. Maybe investing in youth talent – the human capital of our game – is too much of an effort. Or maybe it is time for us to move on from the battlefields of history and the mind-set of the past to the more important question of where the game should go in the future.

One other issue about England must be raised. Money has come to dominate the global game and England is the most extreme, and some would say the most successful, example of this. Club finance in the English Premiership, including those recipients of massive parachute payments when they are relegated, makes the total amount of broadcasting income to the Scottish game seem ridiculously inadequate. So, there is much to envy. But we should resist. There may be a time in the distant future when our game will have value to a European or Global audience and, indeed, to a British and Scottish audience.

Until then, we must accept that we must build a way forward by using the natural talent of Scotland and a wiser use of existing football income and assets to add value to the whole game; this is the cornerstone of every successful organisation. It is also worth remembering that investment in Scottish football has increased over the past two decades but a return on that extra spend is not immediately obvious in parts of the game, especially in relation to youth development, the national game, and our international teams, both male and female.

The Worth of Human Capital

On 6 March 1965, I played my first professional game with East Fife and, at aged 16, was one of the youngest players in the game. The venue was Hampden Park, Glasgow, our opponents were Queens Park and it was a Scottish League 2 fixture. The stadium, looking tired and in need of a face lift, was nevertheless stunning; vast terraces and the home of the famous Hampden roar, steeped in the most amazing football history and the stage upon which some of the greatest games in world football had been played. The game itself did not live up to the iconic location and East Fife lost. We had to play with ten men for virtually the whole match. Substitutes were not yet part of the rules and when Maurice Aitken, our right half, was injured, the rest of the match was an uphill struggle. It is easy to forget how much the game has changed, and for the better. It would inconceivable to think today that an injury and a player going off could ruin a game. What a baptism.

Looking back at my first game raises the questions of age and ability in football. I played in an era where if you were good enough, you were old enough. Times have changed and Scottish football, at least on the surface, seems less welcoming to very young players. Leaving aside, for a minute, the arduous requirements of financial austerity facing the game, is there a youth problem in Scottish football and if so, why should that be? The large numbers of foreign players, especially in the Premiere league, at a level of nearly 54%, is one of the highest amongst the UEFA countries. The attitude of some managers and their preference for the so-called 'finished product' is growing, to the exclusion of young talented Scots. The lack of financial incentives being given to clubs to play young talent is not helping, though I remain puzzled as to why anyone should need an incentive to play young Scots, especially if they have the ability.

A chance meeting five years ago in the Hilton Hotel Glasgow allowed me to meet up with Eddie Gray, a remarkably talented player with Leeds United and now one of their football ambassadors. We both recognised each other and reflected on the past. Had it not been for injuries, he would have become one of the greatest ever Scottish players – he probably is anyway.

When I signed a two-year contract with Leeds 50 years ago, I was in digs with Eddie and three other boys. I can still remember the landlady, Ms Hawkins, and her distinctive Welsh accent. I didn't settle down in Leeds but will always remember her with great affection. My time at Leeds as a raw, working-class boy was inspirational. Don Revie, another great Scottish manager, was a great help. As a schoolboy apprentice professional, you not only trained and played but also had other work to do. Painting the Elland Road stand was one of them and cleaning the boots of Bobby Collins, the great Celtic star, was another. The club were promoted that season into the first division of English football and went on to dominate English football under Revie in the 60s and 70s. Since that period their fortunes have slumped but in my brief spell there I learned a lot about the game and myself. Aston Villa had also offered me a place with them, but I am glad it was Leeds. Life is often a question of what might have been. The majority of the boys who signed with Leeds, that bitterly icy winter in 1963, went on to play at full international level for their country, including Gary Sprake, Dennis Hawkins, Jimmy Greenhoff and, of course, Eddie Gray.

In today's world of elite academies and young people being attached to clubs too early, there is a real danger that education is not given the priority it deserves. For the vast majority of young people being signed for professional clubs, only a handful will make it, so there is an absolute premium on every young person continuing with their education. I was fortunate because after leaving school once, I was able to return to my old school and put ten years of school-work into three years and secure myself a future. It is even more important, faced with the challenges of a modern society and high-tech economy, that a rounded and complete education should be part of the football dream.

Every child has a brain and the capacity to do well. Some children, like me, rejected school for sport but let us also acknowledge that some children, for a variety of reasons, are rejected by schools. Thank goodness there are second-chance opportunities in education, but the best time is the first time.

For working class children, it is best to combine sport and learning. It keeps your options open in a world where getting to the top of football, or any other sport, is fiercely competitive and short lived. Being a very important sports child at school – house captain, tennis and athletics champion and football star – does not necessarily entitle you to become a very important adult. If they can make it in the game of football, while matching that with academic achievement, playing young Scots is not just common sense, but provides the 'football capital' that will give us a return on our investment, for club and country.

These factors taken together represent an immediate crisis of confidence in our talented young people, the undermining of any long-term objective of building a better and more attractive game and an insane and unequal distribution of scarce financial resources.

In my review of Scottish football in 2010, I recommended the setup of a new youth strategy and the creation of youth academies throughout Scotland. I now chair the Fife Academy comprising of the four Fife clubs; Dunfermline, Raith Rovers, East Fife and Cowdenbeath. This has provided me with invaluable insights into the potential and the problems facing our children and young people in building a future in the game.

Unfortunatley, Scotland is not yet in the right place and the tensions between club and country, SPFL and SFA, and the unfair distribution of power and money within the game is seriously holding us back, and allowing other countries to march forward as we collectively fail to understand the enormity of our youth crisis and stubbornly refuse, or are unable to see, the bigger global picture. We have a broken youth player pathway, serious underfunding, no incentives for clubs to think young, too many mediocre foreign players, too much short termism, unbalanced investment, no big ambition and a failure to understand or grasp the demands from our country for success.

The Women's Game: Equal Recognition

The women's game is now an important and vital part of our football and this will become more evident over the next decade. But, more must be done to attract the enthusiasm, skills and ambition of tens of thousands of girls and women who are getting involved at the grass roots level. Equally important is the drive to find, nurture and develop young female talent. The Scottish football male mind-set is changing, but not quickly enough to match the ambition of our current women's game and the pace with which it is developing. Tremendous progress is being made. After qualifying for the European Championships, they are now well placed to progress to the World cup finals. This would be a remarkable achievement and demands greater recognition and resources.

I met the previous women's international coach, Anna Signeul, as part of my review of Scottish football in 2010. We discussed many of the problems facing her game and there was broad agreement that although the game had come a long way, there was still an infinite amount of work still to be done. Part of our long discussion in the Balmoral Hotel in Edinburgh was to convince her that I was on her side. Her battles with the hierarchy of Scottish football had clearly taken their toll but she had done a remarkable job, leaving her successor, Shelley Kerr, a great legacy.

Imagine if we were establishing the SFA this year, instead of in 1873; representing 50% of the population, the women's game would require equal treatment. This of course is not what is happening. The fitness, wellbeing, health and sports agenda is as relevant to young women and girls as it is to young men and boys and indeed this agenda should apply to both sexes and all ages. A greater effort is required to provide more investment, sponsorship and resources as a successful women's game will encourage more young girls to get involved. We must dispel the idea that a woman's place is not on the pitch. The game has to open up and celebrate the fact that women can bring and win success for themselves, for their communities and for their country. It is time we moved forward.

Football Finance

Understandably, the 'big clubs' deserve their share of the national football 'cake', in addition to the rewards and success they have won for themselves. But the uneven distribution of the national income cannot be justified and the success of the few big clubs, important as this is, cannot be at the expense of the many clubs and the national game. Current thinking and the direction of the game in Scotland appears to be the total antithesis of what would be required for the game is to make a comeback.

A closer look at the English game also suggests that large metropolitan areas, significant city populations, breath-taking levels of broadcasting income and a highly competitive and 'glamourous' Premiership are important pillars of their strength and success. But is the English game at the highest level, English in name only? Foreign players are at record levels, not as high as in Scotland, and foreign managers are on the increase. Foreign ownership is growing and foreign money is flowing in. And, as the Chelsea boss has shown, Roman Abramovich, a Russian oligarch, once snubbed, can take his billions to another country – in this case Israel – seek citizenship and threaten to cut the financial pipeline to his club for stadium investment. Who calls the shots? Is global capital finding English football a useful venture, a good place to dump debt, a convenient but short-term investment or a plaything of the fabulously wealthy? Is there such a thing as the soul of the game? Where do the fans fit in? Who runs English Premier League football?

For Scotland, of course, more income would be welcome as many clubs are struggling for survival, not for success. On a much lower level of finance, our game in Scotland is in danger of mimicking the weaknesses of the English game, where the interests of money are distorting the real priorities of the game, discriminating against other investments in the national game and failing to support long-term measures of youth development. We need to answer honestly, the question: Does the national game in Scotland have the same priority as it had 20 years ago? Fine words are no substitute for serious and sustainable investment.

Short-term priorities and a tendency to ignore the 'common football good' in its various guises can be a product of too little finance, as well as too much finance. The way we run our game also determines the friends we can attract and the interest and investment we can generate. Who runs the game and in whose interests is it run, seems pertinent...

We do live in a modern world. The free movement of people, the Bosman Ruling and the removal of restrictions generally in the game, have all contributed to a more fluid and flexible recruiting environment. The game has also benefitted from foreign players. But all of this, boosted by more finance, is squeezing out new home-grown talent and the current path we are on is detrimental to the future of the national side and a huge disincentive to young people seeking to live their dream of club and international football. Foreign players can be an asset and help in many ways, but they can never play for Scotland!

There is an imbalance in the game and there are many practical steps that can be taken to put young people first. Getting a better mix would be easy, but we must change the mind set that currently grips the game. Other countries don't think like us, so why do we when decline is staring us in the face and screaming at us for a shake-up in our approach?

Yes, this was the main recommendations made in my review of Scottish Football in 2010, and the main subject of one of the two reports prepared. But that was nearly a decade ago and we haven't made the progress we should have. Project Brave, the hoped for solution, has been derailed by an indefensible and unfair distribution of money, a lack of ambition and hijacked by clubs who do have a role to play but should not an exclusive role or be financed at the expense of smaller clubs and large parts of Scotland. We do not want any more clubs to join those who are now only entries in the history book.

One of my saddest and eventful trips as a player was to Cathkin Park at Crosshill, Glasgow, to play Third Lanark in the final game of their long and illustrious football life in 1967. The 95-year-old club was about to fold and East Fife were the visitors. I remember the feelings of neglect, tiredness and hopeless inevitability around the pitch and dressing rooms, not helped by the fact that the club was penniless. So much so that I think we brought our light bulbs and soap, just in case the stories we had been told were true. On this day, I was playing left back for East Fife and scored an own goal, scored the equaliser, and then was booked, for what must have been a soft tackle misunderstood by the referee. This was indeed a memorable match for me, just a pity it took place at such a bad time for a great club. One of the first founding members of the game in 1872 had started life as an offshoot of the 3rd Lanarkshire Rifle Volunteers.

The old pitch is still there and the ambitious development plans surrounding the demise of the club over 50 years ago, along with a number of ideas to recreate a successor football club to inherit the once proud record of achievement of Third Lanark came to nothing. So why Third Lanark? I suppose no club is forever. But it is always so unfair when, through no fault of loyal and often long-suffering fans, that the people running the club let them down, get carried away with their own vested and personal interests and betray their trust and loyalty.

Whilst this would certainly help make the case for more serious fan involvement in the running of clubs, it also reinforces the need for financial probity and the need for seriously responsible people to run our clubs, those who have sufficiency of regard for the rich tapestry of traditions, sentiment and decency that are part of Scottish football. Recent events in the game are a brutal reminder of the confusion of identities and the conflicts of interest that can bring clubs down. Money is an invaluable commodity, but also a dangerous one.

Fans are the Lifeblood of the Game

Football has experienced many tragedies and the only silver lining in many of those dark days was the boost given to better conditions for the fans, all seated stadia and the recognition that while there had been great improvements on the pitch, not a lot had been done for fan comfort, convenience and safety.

Since the end of the 1980's there has been a greater recognition of the importance of supporters and their need for safe surroundings, but more needs to be done. Their role as fans goes along side their financing of the game as customers, and we should not forget the history and solidarity they pass from one generation to the next in keeping the game alive and relevant.

Team at the Top

The problems of Scottish football may manifest themselves on the pitch at Hampden and at 42 other club venues throughout Scotland, but they don't start there. Instead, Scotland's problems are routed in the institutions, the culture and out-dated mind-sets of a game that increasingly looks inward for solace and inspiration and, in doing so, is cutting itself off from the very people that can help breathe new life into our national game. It is about ambition. It is about our DNA. It is about self-belief. It is about waking up to what other small population countries – Ireland, Northern Ireland, Wales and Iceland – with wider horizons are telling us, year, after year, after year.

In 2009, I was privileged and honoured to be asked by Gordon Smith, CE of the SFA, and President George Peat, to undertake a comprehensive review of Scottish football. After producing over 100 recommendations from two reports, the findings were well received and the vast majority of them have been implemented. So, the game is in much better shape than it was nearly a decade ago. But what I failed to realise at that time was the real state of the game, the underlying tensions and strains permeating and the impact that cultural, institutional and strategic weaknesses were having on the ability of the game to change and modernise. The official game was paralysed and had become the victim of over a century of inertia and inability to see itself through the prism of what the modern game required if success at club, community and country level, was to be achieved.

Equally important, the game had become detached and disconnected from wider Scotland and, more problematically, its own support and fan base. I remained confused about what the big ambition was, who was expected to provide it and in what form or context was it to be delivered. It looked like a game with many parts but no real inner strength or focus. On reflection, it was ridden with faction football; different strands of special and vested interests vying for power, finance, and opportunity. Change was not a frequent visitor to Scottish Football and the whole game had become unsure of its purpose. Too much power in the hands of a few, too little power in the hands of the many. Democracy had become an alien force in structures that were designed to either respect or manage change effectively. It was never facing up to the scale of the challenge facing the game, especially after the mid-90's where Scottish football fell off a cliff in terms of winning anything in Europe at Club or International level. There was no mechanism for collectively acknowledging weaknesses and thinking through progressive changes. It was isolated, inward looking and very exclusive and there was no acceptance of the need to reach out. A terribly defensive mentality emerged as a coping mechanism that saw very critical friends as critical enemies.

This was the real review that could only be hinted. Politics as the art of the possible had to be the priority and while the list of practical proposals were put forward and accepted, this was not, looking back, the agenda that the game needed at that time. But it is now the basis upon which a wholesale transformation of Scottish football must be undertaken. Change in this context is all about choices and so the first step is for the game is to decide what it wants to be. What does success look like and what are the major issues to tackle? How do we radically reenergise and modernise the strategic, institutional and cultural aspects of football to make it relevant to the 21st century? How do we reconfigure the distribution of power, finance, opportunity and wealth in the closed and closeted corridors of the Hampden Headquarters?

Who is likely to campaign for change and who is likely to resist to safeguard vested interests? Or, is there a way forward that can balance competing interests and secure a Scottish game in which, within certain parameters, there are only winners. But also, in doing so, achieve the greater goal of a game fit for purpose in the 21st century and which restores pride in a powerful national asset.

CHAPTER FIVE

On the International Stage, Falling off a Cliff

WE HAVEN'T QUALIFIED FOR the final stages of a World Cup in 20 years. This has become an enduring truth that has wrapped Scottish football in a shroud since our last appearance in the most important World football tournament in Paris 1998. For the overwhelming majority of Scots today, participating and succeeding at the highest levels of international football has been a source of national pride, ambition and in a way, solidarity in an increasingly divisive society and troubled world. Reflecting both, a previous era where we seemed to be more successful and a future that looks increasingly uncertain, our national embrace of the importance of football is loosening and confidence in our game is being seriously undermined while sentiment and emotion are fast disappearing.

So, what has been happening post-war and to what extent does 20 years of World Cup failure explain the whole narrative of Scotland on the world stage? The answers make uncomfortable reading but also serve to illustrate the deep-seated failures of Scottish football and its long-term decline, not only in the World Cup, but also in the European Championships and European Club competitions. The following tables provide a series of insights from the post-war period to the present, which can best be described as a game of two halves with a dramatic ending.

First, the 'Golden Age' of the 60s, 70s and 80s through to the mid- 90s, when participation in the World Cup and European Club competitions was sustained and successful. For a small country on the eastern edge of Europe subjected to the chill winds of Siberia and the unpredictable Atlantic weather, this was a remarkably enlightened period in Scottish football.

Second, we take a step backward from everything that had gone before. In the 1990s to 2018, qualifying for international tournaments ended and success at club level in Europe disappeared, with two notable exceptions.

In brutal terms, our involvement on the World and European stage ended in 1998, when the Scottish game fell off a cliff and an international football famine set in, from which we have neither escaped nor recovered. Analyses of the Scottish game, especially the excellent BBC's documentary series in 2016, have suggested that there was a tipping point in Scottish football around the '80s/'90s. This is certainly borne out by looking at the tables accompanying this chapter. Leaving aside the domestic game, our international football at both club and national level during this period, pose a challenging set of questions, the answers to which start to explain our decline at a point in time, and in the longer term, may help to address the real problems of Scottish football.

Performance at International Level: 1950 – 2018

European Cup Winner Cup

Fair Cities Cup

UEFA Cup

UEFA Europa League

European Cup

European Champions League

World Cup

Europeans Championships (EUROS)

	Scottish Teams in European Competitions	World Cup	European Championships
1950s	O	✓ (54) ✓ (58)	
1960s	OOOOOO OOOOOO OOOOOO		
1970s	OOOO OO O ★	✓ (74) ✓ (78)	
1980s	OOOO OOOO OO ★	✓ (82) ✓ (86)	
1990s		✓ (90) ✓ (98)	✓ (92) ✓ (96)
2000s	OO		
2010s			
2020s			

O Clubs reaching the Quarterfinals of the Competition

✓ National side reaching final stages (qualifying year in brackets)

★ Super Cup participants

Scottish Clubs in European Competition 1950 – 2018

- European Cup Winners Cup
- Fair Cities' Cup
- UEFA Cup
- Europa League
- Europe Cup
- Champion's League

	Scottish Teams							
Decade	Dundee United	Celtic	Rangers	Dunfermline	Hearts	Hibs	Dundee	Aberdeen
1950		ooo	oooo	ooo		o		
1960		ooo	ooo			ooo	oo	
1970		ooo	ooo (Plus Super Cup)			o		
1980	oooo	o	o		o			oo (Plus Super Cup) o
1990								
2000		o	o					
2010								
2020								

o = Scottish clubs reaching at least the quarterfinals of the tournaments listed above

* Celtic reached the last 16 of Champions League in 2006-7, 2007-8 and 2012-13. After the domination of European competitions by Rangers and Celtic in the '60s and '70s, the 'old firm' were eclipsed by the 'new firm' in the '80s.

World Cup Qualifiers 1950 – 2018
(National Teams – countries with 11 million or less)

National Teams	50	54	58	62	66	70	74	78	82	86	90	94	98	02	06	10	14	18
N. Ireland			✓						✓	✓								
Wales			✓															
Ireland											✓	✓		✓				
Iceland																		✓
Serbia															✓	✓		✓
Denmark										✓			✓	✓		✓		✓
Norway												✓	✓					
Sweden	✓		✓			✓	✓	✓			✓	✓		✓	✓			✓
Portugal					✓					✓				✓	✓	✓	✓	✓
Belgium									✓	✓	✓	✓	✓	✓			✓	✓
Croatia													✓	✓	✓		✓	✓
Scotland		✓	✓				✓	✓	✓	✓	✓		✓					
Switzerland	✓	✓		✓	✓							✓			✓	✓	✓	✓
Austria		✓	✓					✓	✓		✓		✓					
Czech Rep															✓			
Greece																		
Latvia																		
Slovenia														✓		✓		
Slovakia																✓		
Albania																		

✓ = Qualified for the final stages of the World Cup

European Championship Qualifiers 1960 – 2018

Population (Millions)	National Teams	60	64	68	72	76	80	84	88	92	96	00	04	08	12
1.8	N. Ireland														
3	Wales														
4.8	Ireland														
0.35	Iceland														
7	Serbia														
5.7	Denmark		✓					✓	✓	✓	✓	✓	✓		✓
5.3	Norway											✓			
9.9	Sweden									✓		✓	✓	✓	✓
10	Portugal							✓			✓	✓	✓	✓	✓
11.3	Belgium				✓		✓	✓			✓				
4	Croatia										✓		✓	✓	✓
5.5	Scotland			*						✓	✓				
8.7	Switzerland										✓		✓	✓	
8.7	Austria													✓	
10	Czech Rep										✓	✓	✓	✓	✓
11	Greece						✓						✓	✓	✓
1.9	Latvia												✓		
2	Slovenia											✓			
5.4	Slovakia														
2.8	Albania														

✓ = Qualified for the final stages of the European Championship

* = First time Scotland entered

Scotland's failure is one thing, but the success of other countries is equally worrying as it shows that we are not only in absolute decline but also in relative decline. International competitors seem hungry for success and have achieved it in many aspects of the game: the way they play, their confidence, basic ball skills, organisation, discipline, hunger for success, physical strength, ambition, dedication and at times, a superior sense of pride and passion. These qualities are universal and not the sole preserve of big countries. Significantly, population size seems to be no impediment to national success and the ability of nations to win international recognition.

The World Cup in Russia 2018 suggests that countries with a population of less than 11 million people have been successful in qualifying.

Country	Population (millions)
Belgium	11.3
Croatia	4.1
Denmark	5.7
Iceland	0.35
Portugal	10
Serbia	7
Sweden	9.9
Switzerland	8.7

Similarly, if you consider the European Countries that have qualified for the World Cup between 1950 and 2018, who didn't qualify for Russia 2018, and who qualified for the European Championships between 1960 and 2016, they have also experienced success despite their population size. It is one of the enduring myths that small countries do not have the footballing capacity or ambition to succeed at international level. Scotland has talked itself into thinking that size does matter and that being a victim is an easy excuse for our dismal record in the last 25 years.

Country	Population (millions)
Northern Ireland	1.8
Wales	3
Republic of Ireland	4.8
Norway	5.3
Austria	8.7
Czech Republic	10

Greece	11
Albania	2.8
Latvia	1.9
Scotland	5.6
Slovenia	2
Slovakia	5.4

One of the most successful countries, in the period in which we have declined, is Denmark, with a population similar to Scotland; a cold Nordic country that is wealthy, progressive, stable and where poverty is not recognised as a driving force in achieving national footballing success. But it is a country where the focus of national interest, and the top priority for spending, is the national team. The other nation that stands out in this debate about population size, is Iceland, yet another example of a country where climate, social class and wealth are not an obstacle to sporting progress. After their success in the European Championships in 2016 and their defeat of England, they qualified for Russia 2018 and in their first match held Argentina, one of the favourites to win the tournament, to a draw. Their presence on the world stage is nothing short of remarkable, or is it? Somewhere in that country there is an ambition the size of the sun, a capacity to succeed limited only by the individual strengths and weaknesses of the players and a sense of national purpose and cohesion that meaning that small country can deliver. It is important to point out that Uruguay, population of 3.4 million and Albania, population of 2.8 million, have qualified respectively for World Cups and the European Championships. They are hardly house-hold names but have arrived at the top table of World competitions.

World Cup, 1950 – 2018

Post-war Scotland participated in the 1954 and 1958 World Cups. We did qualify for the tournament in 1950 as runners up in the Home Championship but declined because we hadn't won the tournament. This was not a popular decision and there was a great deal of public outcry. After a gap of 16 years, we qualified for the final stages in 1974. As part of this 'Golden Age' we also qualified in '78, '82, '86, '90 and '96. This was a remarkable run of success. Even our adventure in Argentina in 1978 fitted that description. The only time in recorded history that a country had won the World cup before it had started, celebrated the victory before we left for the tournament and then had to endure the most crushing and humiliating defeat. But I have to say that I was one of the millions that was completely caught up in the nostalgia, sentiment, and delusion, and believed that we were on our way with 'Ally's army' to win. No lack of ambition, but thin on realism. But that is the joy of the game, dreaming is okay!

We have qualified for the World Cup eight times out of a possible 18 since 1950, or eight out of 13 up to 1998. Since 1950, of the 20 European countries with less than 11 million population who qualified for the World Cup, only Sweden has a better record than Scotland with ten successful attempts. Belgium and Scotland were successful on eight occasions but Belgium and Sweden kept going after 1998.

After 1998 we just disappeared from the final stages of any World Cup, the equivalent of falling off a football cliff. This is the position today and one that haunts the nation, our devoted fan base and our long-suffering Tartan Army. It is a constant reminder of failure that eats away at our internationalism and our sense of justifiable national pride that was developed and nurtured during a brilliant run of qualifying success in the 'Golden Age'. But our analysis also shows the spectacular progress being made by other countries. While we were in decline, other countries were making progress. Over the last 20 years, Denmark (4 times), Sweden (3), Serbia (3), Belgium (3), Portugal (5), Croatia (4) and Switzerland (4) have all reached the final stages of the World Cup.

Scotland has slumped at a time that other countries have started to ascend, and there is no immediate reason as to why this might change, unless there is a change in mind-set in Scotland and a radical transformation in our attitude towards the national side. Scotland, on the world stage does not seem to be a priority for our game. Consciously or unconsciously, we have downgraded our international side. Other countries have improved, and we have declined. The DNA of post war Scotland, as the basis for young talented Scots, and as evidenced at club and international level in the Golden Age, must still exist but it is not being identified, nurtured, developed, and given the chance. The national game is losing out to the club game. From the second-best qualifier amongst countries under 11 million population in the period 1950–2018, Scotland is now one of the worst. These are hard but revealing facts. We are a country that has lost its way in international football, has no one to blame but itself and has created a confusing and distorting set of priorities that have helped Scotland become a second or third-rate footballing nation.

The European Championships

Our international involvement in the European Championships between 1960 and 2016 is depressing and reveals the harsh reality of a country that has never been enthused or excited by this tournament. In return, Scotland has one of the poorest records of qualifying in its 56-year history and no record at all in this competition in the last 22 years.

Scotland first entered the tournament in 1968 and has only qualified on two occasions, 1992 and 1996, under Andy Roxburgh and Craig Brown. We have failed to qualify for any of the finals between 1996 and 2016, qualifying for only two out of 13 championships. This is a dismal record in a tournament that has seen the qualification of Northern Ireland, Wales, and the Republic of Ireland for the 2016 European Championships, as well as Iceland. Denmark has qualified eight times, including three occasions after 1996, and won in 1992. The performances of those countries with populations of 11 million or less, stands in sharp contrast. In the period, post–1996, the following countries qualified for the finals multiple times; Denmark (3 times), Croatia (4), Sweden (5), Portugal (5), Belgium (2), Switzerland (3), Austria (2) Czech Republic (4), Greece (3), Latvia, Slovenia, Slovakia and Albania (1). Out of 20 countries with populations of 11 million or less, none of them, except Serbia, have failed to qualify for at least one final since 1996, only Scotland. Serbia only arrived on the international scene after the collapse of Yugoslavia.

The obvious question that must be posed time after time; what's wrong with Scotland? Out of 31 European and World Cup tournaments between 1950 and 2018, we have qualified on ten occasions. Out of ten European and World Cup tournaments between 1996 and 2018, we haven't qualified for any of them. The only conclusion to be drawn is that the national team is not the priority it used to be, before the Scottish game became so engrossed in the interests of the club game (mainly the current top five), the arrival of more money, the obsession with the interests of the Premiere League after its creation and a slump into the complacency and contentment of domestic football. This helps explain our diminishing fortunes at international level after 1998, but it does leave open the question as to why we so dismally failed in the European Championships before 1996, especially when we had the players that created our 'Golden Age', available to us and we did incredibly well in the World cup qualifiers in the same period.

Looking forward, there are exemplars for Scotland to learn from. At one level, Denmark and Sweden have been very successful in qualifying for both the World Cup and the European Championships. They also have had levels of further success in the competitions themselves, the final for Denmark in 1992 and semi-final for Sweden in 1958. But both are cold countries and wealthy, where indoor facilities are essential to their national game. These countries are superbly organised and have a forward-looking and expansive approach to their football. Their relationships with outside bodies are more extensive and respectful. Their style is uncompromising and disciplined. Their strengths are energy, fitness, and commitment. Their governance is modern, ambitious, and less bogged down with narrow special interests. Their national game is their number one priority. The legacy of history does not burden their mind set or ambition.

Scotland has also to be aware of countries like Ireland, Northern Ireland and Wales who have less elaborate league structures that require so much time money and effort, and are instead able to concentrate on the bigger picture of the national side and ensure it is given top priority within the game. Serbia, Slovakia, Iceland and even Albania complete the threat to Scotland. Countries that were on the margins of the game are now inside and taking few lectures from anyone. But, they are fast learners and without the self-imposed constraints of the Scottish game, are able to move quickly on the field, have modern governance, the ability to adapt to change and not be weighed down by old cultures and institutional inertia.

The importance of international football cannot be overstated as UEFA embarks on a new Nations League with the intention of removing most of the friendly matches and replacing them with competitive football. There is also a looming battle between UEFA and FIFA as the world body of football attempts to steal the idea of the Nations League, start a new competition and introduce an expansion of the club World Cup. Each of its federations from South America to Africa will be instructed to create their own Nations League. The winner of these continental competitions will play in a global 'final eight' tournament, every four years. These are money-making ideas for a game that is obsessed with riches for the few and scraps for the many. But that need not detain us at this point. What the activities of FIFA and UEFA clearly demonstrate is that there will be much more international football for clubs and countries as we move forward. The new model for the 2020 European Championships will see Scotland host matches as well as seeking to qualify. A successful Scotland could look forward to more competitions at international level, more income for the national game and more encouragement of national fervour, pride, and passion. Success could mean so much. There is a massive incentive to build the national game. There will also be more opportunities at the highest levels of the club game in Scotland. The new structure for the 2020 European Championships will see Scotland host matches, as well as seeking to qualify.

Scottish Clubs in European Competitions

Scottish club success in Europe has been remarkable, record breaking, consistent, inspiring, and entertaining. But with two notable exceptions, Celtic and Rangers appearances in the finals of the UEFA Cup in 2003 and 2007, this all happened in the 'Golden Age', between the 1960s and the end of the 1980s. Since then there has been a dearth of club success in Europe, in sharp contrast to the achievements of earlier years.

Analysis of the six decades of Scottish club participation in Europe, from the '60s to '80s, reveals a similar pattern to Scotland's involvement in the World Cup and the European Championships. The attached table graphically illustrates the history of the game. Since 1960 European competition has taken many forms, including the Inter Cities Fairs Cup, the UEFA Cup, the European Cup Winners Cup and the European Cup, giving way in modern times to the European Champions League and the UEFA Europa League Cup. Each circle on the diagram represents a successful outcome for Scottish clubs participating in European competitions measured by their ability to reach at least the quarterfinals of any of the European tournaments: in the changing world of European club football, it seems reasonable to set the quarterfinals as a useful measure of achievement. Accepting the fact that the tournaments are tougher and more competitive in the modern era.

Today, club opportunities are constrained by our failures over the past 20–30 years to make progress in European competitions. This is the result of the UEFA coefficient system, which cumulatively punishes clubs and nations that don't perform and gives them less priority in qualifying for the Champions League and the UEFA Europa League. Due to the relatively poor performances by most Scottish clubs in recent competitions, clubs enter at the earliest qualifying stage. Consistent underachievement, failure to progress in tournaments, lower coefficients for clubs and country, fewer European qualifying spots and more qualifying rounds form a vicious cycle of decline. Being consistently successful on the European stage, at both club and national level is more than a boost for the fans and it is vital for our credibility as a footballing nation.

After being invited, Hibs were the first Scottish club to participate in European football on the 14 September 1955. The high points of European competition were in the '60s and '70s, which were dominated by the 'old firm' of Celtic and Rangers, and in the 1980s, by what was regarded at that time as the new firm', of Aberdeen and Dundee United.

First, in order of importance, was Celtic winning the European Cup in 1967, the first British club to do so with a team of local players brought up within a few miles of this great club and managed by one of the giants of Scottish football, Jock Stein. This was Scotland's finest becoming Europe's finest. This was a remarkable achievement and another powerful illustration of the ability of Scottish football to win at the highest level and the most important club trophy in the world. This was their only victory in a European competition but they secured many more appearances in finals and semi-finals of other European competitions. Although less significant than a quarter-final, Celtic managed to appear in the last 16 of the Champions League in 2006–7, 2007–8 and 2012–13.

Second, Rangers were very successful in the '60s and '70s and participated in a remarkable number of quarter-finals, semi-finals, and finals. Their greatest achievement was to win the European Cup Winners Cup in season 1971–2. They also appeared in the final of the European Cup Winners cup in 1960–1 and 1966–7.

Third, Aberdeen, managed by Alex Ferguson, won the European Cup Winners Cup in 1983 and in the same year won the European Super Cup. Interesting to note that all the players in the squad were Scottish, as were the Rangers and Celtic cup-winning teams. Changed days! It seemed at that point, the 'new firm' of Aberdeen and Dundee United had broken through. Dundee United were also participating at the highest level of European football and had an interesting skirmish with Barcelona in 1987. United triumphed 3-1 on aggregate, beating Barcelona in both legs, to then progress to the last four and then the final of the UEFA Cup.

An article in the Guardian in February 2016 summed up the astonishing history of Scottish football, under the banner headline of, 'Never mind England in 1966, here's Scotland conquering Europe in 1967'. We were reminded that in that remarkable year, Celtic won five competitions, including the European Cup, Dundee United beat Barcelona home and away, Rangers made it to the Cup Winners Cup final and the national team beat England at Wembley. Was this the high point of Scottish football?

Other clubs have also played their part in the 'Golden Age' of European involvement such as Dunfermline, Hearts, Hibs and Dundee. Lest we forget, there have been great football nights in Europe:

Year	Team and Result
1967	Celtic 2 - 1 Inter Milan
1983	Aberdeen 2 - 1 Real Madrid
1972	Rangers 2 - 1 Bayern Munich
1987	Barcelona 1 - 2 Dundee United
1962	Dundee 8 - 1 Cologne
1970	Celtic 2- 1 Leeds United
1961	Hibs 3- 2 Barcelona
1962	Dunfermline 6- 2 Valencia
1995	Bayern Munich 2- 1 Raith Rovers
1992	Leeds United 1 - 2 Rangers

At club level there have been enormous changes in the scale, importance, and financing of European competitions. Celtic and Rangers have been unable to retain their involvement at such a high level, post-1980s. It is important that we retain our interest in Europe and ensure that at least the five big clubs maintain their competitiveness, big match ambition, demanding skill and fitness levels and have great, young, Scottish players to pick from. In the 'Golden Age', home grown talent was available; the Celtic story is as inspiring as it was successful. The best teams that have ever played in Scotland were also big teams in Europe at that time. Accepting that the footballing world and society have undergone dramatic changes over the past generation, there can be no disputing the basic truth that young talent is the wealth of our game, it is our football capital, and from that investment, there will be a significant return at all levels of the game.

The facts speak for themselves. After a golden period of success at club level in Europe, a long and sustained involvement in the final stages of the World Cup and a dismal record of qualifying for the European Championships, Scottish football today is simply not good enough. Other clubs and countries in Europe have advanced with both bigger ambitions and more sophisticated technical ability. Our international presence has dramatically diminished and despite our history and achievements, Scotland has become a shadow of its former footballing self. Other countries have taken their international game more seriously than us. They have refused to allow their club game to dominate at the expense of their national side. Scottish football has let Scotland down in a manner that would have been unimaginable 25 years ago. There are simply no excuses that can explain away our decline. Our supply of talent should not have evaporated. A country with such deep-seated football DNA should not have fallen off a cliff in the mid- 90s. Other countries have faced social, economic, industrial and political change and have also seen football transform itself, but they have been able to adapt to changing circumstances and still win success. Scottish football has been unable to do this. Why? There are three compelling reasons for this.

First, the importance of the national game has suffered at the expense of the club game. Also, despite changes to our youth policy post-2010, we still do not have a world-class elite academy structure. Finally, our game is inward-looking and is highly protective of narrow self- interests, which is reflected in the uneven and unfair distribution of finance and power and a failure to engage the rest of Scotland in the business of football.

A Short-Term Mind-Set

The manager of the Scotland international team has always been a coveted job, and rightly so. The post carries with it enormous kudos, despite putting you in the firing line of the most energised and hostile media as well as a long suffering public desperate for success on the international stage but who are often disappointed. In the post-war period, there have been many impressive teams and well-qualified mangers, seeking success but never being able to take Scotland beyond the group stages of international competitions.

Surprisingly, and recognising the importance of the post, very few managers have been allowed to remain in the job for long periods. Defeat or failure to qualify for important tournaments has often led to early dismissal or resignation. This may be the same in other countries, but Scotland does seem to have had an incredible turnover of mangers and not necessarily leading to improved performances or international success.

From 1872 to 1953, and 1954 to 1957, there was no official manager or coach, the team was selected by an SFA committee. The role of manager was first established in May 1954 with the appointment of Andy Beattie, who took charge on a part-time basis while continuing as the manager of Huddersfield Town. Beattie was in charge of the team when they qualified for the 1954 World Cup but it would appear that the SFA only allowed him to select a travelling party of 13 players. The official story suggests that this made it impossible for him to perform his duties, so he resigned during the tournament. Scotland were eliminated after a 7-0 drubbing by Uruguay. Behind the scenes, a number of people suggested that Beattie was annoyed that a large contingent of SFA officials and their wives had attended the finals, at great cost, and this is why he resigned.

In the 64 years, from 1954 to 2018, Scotland has had 26 managers, three of them serving on two occasions; Andy Beattie, Jock Stein and Alex McLeish. The longest serving managers, and some would argue the most successful, are Andy Roxburgh and Craig Brown, serving 16 years between them. This means the average time in post was less than 2 years, 5 months. But if you take away the 16 years of Roxburgh and Brown, 24 managers have served a total of 48 years or, on average, 2 years each. This, by any accounts, is a staggeringly small amount of time to be in post if long-term planning, continuity and sustainable success are to be achieved. This is short-termism at its worst. Different circumstances will dictate why a person takes the job, where in their career it may fit and how the availability of a club post is a more attractive position to have. But should the cycle of qualifying for the European Championship and the World Cup be the main determinant of who fills the position of manager and for how long?

Nevertheless, the Scottish job is of significance, but are the managers being picked for the right reasons. What constitutes the best credentials for the job? Are we looking for a coach or a manager? Is the time frame we are offering making any sense? More importantly, why should the post be so firmly fixed to the short-term goal of qualifying for either the World Cup or the European Championships? The spectacle of blood-letting, scapegoating or seeking a sacrifice are well-worn social rituals but may, in the long term, be wasteful and of little consequence. Imagine what would happen if an SFA committee were still in charge of the Scottish team, including selection. To what extent should a manager be held to account when the rest of the

Scottish game is not? Why are the senior officials of the SFA committees dealing with investment and finance not being held to account for 20 years of failure to qualify for a World Cup? Why after 20 years of international footballing failure are those elected officials responsible for youth policy not asked to account for our inability to have more elite young Scottish players performing in our national squads? Who is ultimately responsible for the failure of Scottish football on the international stage? And why do we just remove managers without there being searching questions asked of the culture, the institutions, and the ambition of those responsible for delivering success? This is supposed to be a team effort.

Scottish football, like Scottish life, finds it easy and convenient to have a ready-made excuse for every disappointing occasion. This avoids too much heart-searching or scratching of heads and leads inevitably to past mistakes being repeated. Any Scottish football manager is responsible for the players and the performance on the pitch but collectively all of those associated with the game are responsible for the quality he must work with. It would be helpful if every manager had the talent, skills, stature and near superhuman qualities of Alex Ferguson, Matt Busby and Jock Stein, but they don't. These are very different times! Personalities do matter, but the modern game needs structures, strategies, and sustainable policies within which managers or coaches can create long-term success and keep building for the future. Short-term thinking is ruining our game.

Foreign Players

Football reflects the globalised world we live in and from which we undoubtedly benefit. The general flow of players and the influx from other countries into Scotland is to be welcomed. In many instances, they enrich our game and make it a much more enjoyable spectacle for the fans. Diversity in the game is important and it works for us in two ways, with Scottish players playing abroad and in the 'home' countries as well. The only danger is that when the percentage of foreign players reaches a certain level, the Scottish game runs the risk of limiting opportunities for young talented Scots. Although figures are subject to change, over 50% of the Scottish Premiere League comprises foreign players. Scotland and England are amongst the European countries with the highest levels. Some of these players are undoubtedly talented and bring new dimensions to our game, but others less so.

This gives rise to the obvious question; why are so many Scottish managers determined to sign players from abroad who have less than inspiring contributions to make to our national game? There are also wider questions. Are we producing enough young Scottish players and if so are they being given the opportunity to play and express their worth? Are too many clubs and coaches looking to buy the finished product from outside Scotland, instead of developing home grown talent, which for them may be costly and time-consuming? Are we providing enough incentives for clubs and scepti-cal managers to take on youth talent and get them to the next level? Why haven't we initiated some research into this?

Many issues in football are inextricably linked. It is hard to believe but the reluctance of clubs to take on youth talent, our growing capacity to buy foreign players and our hesitating approach to the development of elite tal-ent in Scotland are undermining the quality of our international teams and sending out the wrong message about the future of Scottish football. If the finished article is so important to Scottish Premier clubs, why are we not doing more with our own talent? There is one truth amidst this conjecture about developing our youth talent. Foreign players may or may not enrich our game, but they will never play for Scotland. This is a good reason to think positively. This is not about abandoning foreign players, it is about giving our young players in Scotland more opportunity and priority, repre-senting as it does, one of the best ways to inspire young players and improve the performance of Scottish international teams in the future. The system increasingly looks like it is rigged against them.

The world of football has changed dramatically over the past 60 years. The international stage has experienced the two faces of Scotland. During the period from the 1970s to the mid-90s, Scotland routinely qualified for the World Cup and despite failing to move on from the group stages in any of them, we showed a consistency of effort and a determination to display the pride and passion of a football-mad country. In sharp contrast, the 1990s showed a Scotland being left behind. This in turn has reduced our credibility as a serious football country, damaged our reputation and depressed the expectations of loyal fans; not withstanding the fact that our country and a dedicated and incredibly patient fan-base, stands ready to rally around the national team, if only things could be different. Their commitment is not being matched by the leaders of the Scottish game where the whole interna-tional team effort is being undervalued, undermined and losing out to the interests of the club game.

Our analysis has revealed that a combination of factors has made a huge impact on Scotland's ability to compete at the highest level. Why was this allowed to happen? More to the point, why, when faced with obvious failures, have the football authorities not embraced a new and transformative approach? This doesn't require an Einstein level of think-tank consideration. Clubs matter to communities and country. The success of Rangers, Celtic and Aberdeen at the highest level of European football was good for our national psyche, our international success and status. Why didn't we see the growth in the number of countries competing on the international stage? Why didn't we appreciate the new reality of countries rapidly developing their football infrastructure? Why didn't we take the corrective steps necessary to maintain our challenge at this level? Why as more countries competed on the international stage, did we not appreciate the threats this posed to our decades of achievement?

Scottish Players in the Top League

Only six countries in UEFA have a worse record than Scotland in playing foreign nationals in our top league. Currently in the Scottish Premiership, 46% of nearly 300 players in the Scottish Premiership are Scottish and 54% are foreign. This was the subject of an excellent piece of journalism in the *New York Times* and supplementary analysis in *The Scotsman* and *Daily Record*.

An increasingly global and cosmopolitan game has changed the face of Scottish football. No one expected to see the 96% of Scottish-born players in our leagues in the '60s changed in such a dramatic fashion. This is a worrying issue considering that indigenous talent is our only way to international success. The Bosman Rule changed everything and accelerated the trend towards foreign players but this does not explain why Scotland was one of the countries leading the European pack. This is another piece of the jigsaw that helps explain why, with the advent of the Scottish Premiership in 1998, we fell of a football cliff and since then have failed to qualify for the World Cup or the European Championships.

Jean Marc Bosman, a Belgian professional, launched a legal challenge against RFC Liege over their refusal to sell him to a French club. He was successful in this landmark case. FIFA immediately recognised the danger and in 2008, created the 6/5 rule, requiring teams in the top tiers to start with at least six domestic players in league matches with the aim of retaining national identity. Unfortunately, this was rejected by the European Parliament who argued that it was inconsistent with the four freedoms that were laid down in the Single Market.

This is now a full-blown crisis and another serious wake up call for those of us who care deeply and passionately about the failure of the national side. One of the main aims for my review of Scottish Football in 2010 was to recognise the fact that our reservoir of talent was drying up and to address this sorry state of affairs. However, nearly a decade on, my frustration remains as we fail to capture either the scale of the crisis or the urgency of resolving the matter. There is no future for us in club or country involvement in Europe or worldwide if we continue to drag our feet over the youth crisis. Our international reputation is poor at present.

Recent research suggests that the Scottish Premiership has, 'more players from England's lower leagues and cheap imports from other countries'. It is disturbing to read in the *New York Times* that, 'nowhere is this vast power shift in global soccer landscape seen more clearly than in the Scottish Premiership!' Surveys from February 2017 suggest that within the shocking overall figure of 46%, there are considerable variations between clubs in Scotland ranging from Inverness Caley with 28% Scots-born to St Johnstone who have 80%.

But post-Bosman, there are again questions for our clubs and the Scottish Premiership, as to why they pursued foreign players with such vigour and failed to retain and strengthen Scottish identity in our game, a choice which is now having such devastating consequences for young Scots, whose opportunities to play at the highest levels are being severely restricted. So why are we selling so many talented young Scots short? A football agent – another wasteful area of football expenditure – told BBC Scotland,

> The English Premier has grown and blossomed into the principal football competition in the World. It is regarded as the Holy Grail and Scotland's proximity means that we are able to offer players a platform where they could come and perform; somewhere that was a hop, skip and a jump from England's top league.

Foreign players should have the opportunity to play in Scotland. That is not the question. It is a matter of balance. We can't neglect Scottish talent. This is short termism at it's worst. The short-term fix means we are destroying long-term opportunities to rebuild our international reputation. The more we rely on imports, the less interested we are in nurturing Scottish talent. This attitude is far too prevalent and is becoming part of the mind-set of the game. Project Brave is not an optional extra but represents a key component of breaking down our resistance to young Scots and giving them real opportunities.

Origins of Young Players

Some other research, prepared by one of our leading football coaches and still a work in progress, reveals the origins of young talent as measured by looking at the players who won their first international cap for Scotland in the period from 1998 to 2016. Nearly 70 players pulled the Scottish jersey over their heads for the first time in the period between 1998 and 2016. The origins of their route to success, not necessarily the clubs they were playing for when they first played for Scotland, provide a valuable and surprising insight into the role played by Scottish clubs during this period.

Of the 72 players:

- 49 from Scottish clubs, the main contributors: Celtic 6, Rangers 8, Dundee 4, Dundee United 2, Hearts 5, and Hibs 7

- 14, or less than 20%, from the Old Firm

- 35 from the rest of Scotland

- 32 from Edinburgh, Glasgow, and Dundee

- 23 from England.

There is a significant spread of talent, but possibly fewer from Rangers and Celtic than might have been expected. The figures also shed some light on other parts of Scotland and other clubs from all four divisions that should be doing more, but are likely to be excluded from the current arrangements for Project Brave.

In other European countries, there appears to be a more concerted effort to combine identity, youth development and foreign nationals into a more coherent offering to the fans. But not in Scotland. In Spain, they have a lower percentage of imported players than many of its peers among European top leagues. There is an abundance of talent to be found locally, schooled in the natural style of play. Similarly, in Germany, after a great deal of soul searching at the start of the millennium, huge reforms were introduced to develop local talent and equally important, to encourage teams to use them. This is sadly lacking from the Scottish game where there are few incentives to use young people and little exhortation from the centre, in the form of the SFA, to do so. This is where country over club becomes a vital expression of Scotland's national interest.

The Bundesliga's youth is now one of the central planks of the marketing of the game and its appeal. Scotland should learn the lessons of others and strive not only for a transformation of attitude but to symbolise youth as a new era in Scottish football where the celebration of elite young Scots becomes the cornerstone of our future success.

Foreign Footballers Playing in Scotland

Assessing the quality of foreign players in Scotland is difficult. But one measure could be the numbers of foreign players with Scottish clubs who performed for their own international sides in the World Cup in Russia 2018. Only seven players were involved from six countries: Mikael Lustig. Tom Rogic, Dedryck Boyata, Cristian Gamboa, Bruno Alves, Kari Arnason and Jamie MacLaren. The numbers have changed little for the World cups since 1998: 2018 – 7 players, 2014 – 4 players, 2010 – 8 players, 2006 – 8 players, 2002 – 7 players and 1998 – 3 players.

Over the last 20 years, 37 players from Scottish clubs have played for their national sides in the World Cup. Scotland is not attracting more foreign players, good enough to play for their own countries, acknowledging the fact that there may be other players in Scotland who are internationalists but whose countries have never qualified for the World cup in recent times. This provides evidence to the effect that there maybe many reasons why Scottish clubs buy more foreign players than other countries, but the highest quality of international talent may not be the most important consideration. Why so few Scots?

Finding talent is one thing, using it is another. A strategy, for constructing a conveyor belt of youth talent (of both sexes), requires many approaches. Crucially, short termism is the scourge of Scottish football and is deeply damaging to any sense of national ambition and international success. We don't seem to be learning from the successful, we keep repeating the mistakes of the past and a succession of non- appearances at the highest levels of international football have made no impact on the game: this is where the slide of the SFA and its loss of authority is so marked.

- There are no incentives from the SFA for clubs to invest in youth
- There is no world class youth strategy in place
- There is too much reliance on the 'we need the finished product' mind-set

- There are too many foreign players
- There is no Scotland wide approach
- There is too little influence exerted by the SFA and, too much free market football thinking on the part of the clubs!
- There is an urgent need to reassess the number and quality of foreign players in Scotland

On the one hand, we may have all the excuses in the world, Bosman, the Single Market, Globalisation, European Court of Justice, the free movement of people and smart agents, but Scottish clubs don't need to buy foreign players, it isn't compulsory. Bosman gives the players rights of movement, but it does not place an obligation on Scottish clubs to be among the most active in Europe buying them. Scotland can change. Our obsession, with foreign players to the obvious disadvantage of homegrown talent, is entirely voluntary. Again, we have no excuses. Buy global, ignore local is made in Scotland.

The number of foreign players, the origins of our first capped since 1998 and the number of foreign players in Scotland playing for their countries at international level, provide more compelling evidence about our attitude towards elite talent and youth development. Our Golden Age of football was a remarkable period when Scottish talent was in abundance and the conveyor belt of young Scots was enriching the game, north and south of the border. Maybe there was an excuse for our complacency at the end of the Golden Age, in that we didn't see it coming or we thought it would last forever. What we are guilty of is doing nothing about it. Twenty years on from falling off a cliff in the mid-1990s, we don't seem to be going anywhere.

There are a number of compelling reasons behind this state of affairs, which I will discuss later, but three obvious issues are crucial to understanding our demise as a respected international team. The first is that our 'golden football age' was marked by towering managers and a conveyor belt of Scottish talent . If we could produce such quality human capital, especially players, decades ago then why can't that happen now? The DNA of generations can't simply be flushed from the system, but our will to win and succeed can be. The next issue is the overwhelming changes introduced by the new Scottish Premiere League in 1998 and the impact of finance and broadcasting on the game along with the intensification of power and authority in the hands of a very few clubs. This sealed the fate of the National team and in the process started to eat away at the authority of the SFA and increase tensions between club and country; issues which have not been resolved and instead, have got steadily worse. Finally, the way we play our game seems increasingly relevant to the debate on how Scotland should move forward. The 2018 World Cup has revealed significant insights into the different styles of football being played at the highest level. There are many different examples, but there are two that stand out.

First the Russia, Switzerland and Iceland model, where fitness, discipline, strength, toughness, organisation and physicality dominate, with varying level of football skills. Second is the Latin model where emphasis is on basic ball skills, intricate networking, patient build up, and the quick strike. This an example of football being a mind game but carried out with legs and feet. Gordon Strachan touched on this when he talked about physicality and DNA when speaking to the media on leaving the Scotland job. Maybe in a different context his comments would have made more sense.

How does the Scotland team play the beautiful game? Does Scotland capture a bit of both styles of play, or neither of them? Both styles can be successful, but for purists like me the Latin style is more entertaining. The way we play has been nurtured and shaped for decades and is probably an old-fashioned hybrid of what is currently on display in Russia. Our style of play would be difficult to change, but it is a debate worth pursuing as there maybe lessons to be learned. Our game finds it hard to listen, learn and adapt to change and it urgently needs the critical infrastructure, independent or in-house, to think our way ahead and embrace new solutions.

CHAPTER SIX

The Golden Age

Early History

WHEN A NATION HAS more memories than dreams, we have reached a disappointing but significant point in our evolution. This is where Scottish football is today. The problems and challenges of the present overwhelm us and are much more difficult to comprehend because of a 'Golden Age' for club and country just a generation ago, when a great game flourished at European Club level and in World Cup competitions. But our history of the game goes much further back. Football is both ancient and modern.

DD Bone in his *Scottish Football Reminiscences and Sketches*, published in 1890 wrote,

> In Scotland, so closely associated with traditional lore, and the acknowledged birth place of romance and patriotic song, it would be almost dangerous to incur displeasure by attempting to refer to the early history of anything associated with the amusements or recreations of the people, without actually touching on tradition – a point held by some in far greater regard and reverence than, actual fact. Under these circumstances then, I do not want to run the risk of complete annihilation by ignoring the traditional, and even territorial, aspect of football. That the game was played as early as the tenth century, there is any amount of authentic evidence to show, and that it continued to be one of the chief recreations of the people there can be no doubt.

Sir Walter Scott, who previously described football as his favourite Border sport, was also quoted in the same publication.

> Then strip, lads, and to it, though cold be the weather,
> And if by mischance, you should happen to fall,
> There are worse things in life than a tumble on heather,
> For life is itself, but a game at football.

Before getting carried away by Sir Walter's comments, football was at the point of distancing itself from being able to carry the ball with both hands, as the sport of Rugby emerged. But his comments, in a curious way, chime with the insights of Bill Shankly, when talking about football being more important than life or death.

King James I, in 1424, outlawed the playing of it in the 'Football Act 1424' with historical reference being made to 'fute-ball'. This was because of the disruption to military training and its violent nature, which he described as 'a rough and violent exercise'. Subsequent kings issued very similar decrees. James VI was concerned about the violent nature of the game and debarred it from what he described as 'commendable exercise'. Violence was endemic, and the Scottish kings had good reason to issue so many decrees. The Scottish Parliament in 1656 outlawed 'boisterous games' on the Lords Day. Of significance for today's legislators, the James I ban was not repealed until 1906; thank goodness the nation ignored the ban for nearly 500 years!

The Game Gets Started

The first ever rules of Association football were established in London in 1863 by the FA. Scottish clubs started to be formed in the 1860s when the oldest club outside England, Queens Park was set up and played in the English FA Cup, reaching the final twice. At this point, football rules in Scotland still allowed the ball to be handled, whereas in England only the goalkeeper was allowed to handle. By 1870–1, the first match between England and Scotland had taken place at the Oval in London, but this game was not recognised by FIFA as official. Official recognition came a year later.

By this time the game in Scotland was gaining momentum, with the Scottish Cup, the second oldest cup competition in the world, and the SFA both established in 1873. There were many Scottish players in England where payments became legal in 1885. They were given the title of 'Scotch Professors'; maybe this was a hint at the quality of player that would eventually grace so many of the top clubs in England in the 20th century! Reinforcing the invaluable issue of DNA, the Liverpool football team was formed in 1892 with 11 Scots. In theory at least, amateur status existed in Scotland until 1893.

Another significant event was the formation of the Scottish Football League in 1890. Dumbarton and Rangers were named joint champions of the first league. After 1872, Scotland played matches exclusively against the three other home countries with the British Home Championship being established in 1884. This annual meeting of the four home nations was to play an important role in the development of international football, not only as a very competitive tournament, but also as a step to qualify for entry to post-war World Cup competitions. It is worth reflecting on the Scotland versus England battles which dominated domestic football in the period from 1872-1984, when the Home Championship ended and between 1984-1989, when the game was played for the Rous Cup. These epic struggles were firmly rooted in the history of Britain; the real wars and battles that had taken place between the two countries creating a growing sense of nationalism, a defence of national pride and identity and a tendency to blame England for all our national woes and anxieties. There is no doubt in my mind that we wasted too much emotional energy over this very special fixture in the football calendar. Beating England may have become a distraction from pursuing wider international success. But what a fixture it was.

Looking back over nearly 80 years, the top ten attendances for the Scottish National Team have all been against England at Hampden Park. Nearly 1.4 million people watched these games and they remain world records; these are truly astonishing attendance figures and speak volumes about the importance of football in the lives of Scots.

Attendance for Scotland vs. England at Hampden Park

Year	Score (Scotland – England)	Attendance
1937	3 – 1	149,415
1939	1 – 2	149,269
1970	0 – 0	137,438
1948	0 – 2	135,376
1954	2 – 4	134,544
1952	1 – 2	134,504
1933	2 – 1	134,170
1968	1 – 1	134,000
1950	0 – 1	133,300
1964	1 – 0	133,245

The biggest drubbing at the hands of the English was 9-3 in 1961. The biggest drubbing for the English at the hands of the Scots was 7-2 in 1872. And probably the finest year of the 'Golden Age' was 1967 when we beat the World Champions, England at Wembley 3-2. Jim Baxter was the tormentor-in-chief and Scotland played with a flair that has rarely, if ever, been surpassed on the international stage. Celtic became the first British club to win the European Cup and break the Latin grip on the game. Let's remind ourselves that this was Scotland!

Before and After the War Years

The 'Golden Age' of Scottish football between the 60s and the mid-90s came after a very productive and successful late '40s and '50s, which were characterised by an explosion of interest in the game, growing attendances, strong leagues and a much more open access to trophies for a range of clubs; access which simply doesn't exist today. One club, my old club, East Fife illustrates what was taking place prior to the Great War, during the inter-war years and the immediately after the Second World War. Much of this is personal to me, but it was a time in football history when there was creativity, dynamism, working-class support and innovation. There was also a massive outpouring of goodwill for a game that provided some respite from war, industrial decline, poverty, and the inhuman conditions of many work places, including mining, where conditions before the mines were taken into public ownership, were primitive.

The rise of East Fife as a successful, trophy-winning football team is significant example of what was happening in similar mining communities throughout Scotland where managers, teams, fans and players were building the foundations for the best days of Scottish football that still lay ahead. East Fife had been formed in 1903 and my grandfather joined them in 1909, and played until 1913. But before then, he was gripped by the explosion of interest in the game as well as the desire to create new clubs. From the archives, I have him pictured with some of his colleagues standing by a large hamper basket with the name 'Methil Thursday' on it. They had just created a club, as many others were doing in the area. There were not enough clubs to satisfy the demand from young people and children who wanted to be involved. Scotland today has thousands of clubs and this is due, in part, to the early years of the game where the spirit of adventure was alive and active. Before that, my grandfather had played for a team called Navajo Indians. Working down the pits was an unenviable task and on the Saturday of the game, he worked in the morning, lying on his back, hewing coal in a 12-inch seam for nearly ten hours, showered and then went to play. He loved the game.

The second part of the East Fife story concerns the Scottish Cup. Playing in the second division of Scottish football in the 1937–8 season, East Fife became the first team from the second division to win the Scottish Cup, and remain only one of two teams to achieve this. In the cup run, they played in front of nearly 400,000 people, including nearly 200,000 East Fife and Kilmarnock fans who attended the final and the replay. Not only was this a huge achievement but also in seasons 1947–8, 1948–9 and 1953–4 they won the Scottish League Cup, a feat of three victories only bettered by three clubs in the lifetime of Scottish football. For good measure they were Scottish Cup finalists in 1948–9 and lost to Rangers. This was the third part of an incredible story.

Shining the spotlight on East Fife only serves to bring into focus what would have been happening throughout Scotland, possibly not achieving the same type of success in a decade, but many clubs in similar communities were succeeding and achieving. This trilogy of East Fife stories helps illustrate the vibrancy and passion of a football-mad country and as this was happening through out the country, it helped create the base for a golden era to begin in the '60s.

Football was competitive. Crowds were big and enthusiastic. Self-belief took you a long way. Money wasn't everything – indeed great players at the time were paid a pittance – but team success, fan support, club success, player pride and community ambition were important.

In the early '50s and '60s, this complex mix of old industrial structures, political change, a society emerging from the ravages of war and the rebuilding of a new economy boosted the game and provided a positive focus within communities. Large crowds were the order of the day and, again on a personal note, how could East Fife attract crowds of over 20,000, when Methil, and its surrounding area, only had a population of thirty thousand? But this was not just an east coast phenomenon, this was happening throughout Scotland.

The game was creating the foundations for a 'Golden Age of football in the '60s, '70s and '80s and at this point in the evolution, fans and spectators mattered. In addition to their loyalty, they financially supported the game. There was no broadcasting income, players were paid very little and there was a wholesome quality to the game. It may have lacked complex team formations, sophisticated game plans and the deployment of cynical techniques, but there was quality football, played with passion, pride and a sense of humility that is often sadly lacking in the modern game. For players, money was not the driving force, but playing for your community and your country. It would be easy to get carried away with the sentiment, nostalgia, and possible delusion of a different world that existed more than 60 years ago. But, these qualities and values that emerged in a different era are timeless, and their relevance shouldn't diminish as we celebrate the best of modern football. This is a legacy worth preserving.

The Golden Age

The remarkable success of Scottish football in this generation was real and inspiring and it reminds us, in darker times, of what this country is capable of. A different set of social, economic and industrial factors were influencing the game and the country. That's true. Some would argue that this period of Scottish football was shaped by unique forces that could never be replicated or matched in modern times. Why, should this be true? We tend to dismiss the lessons of history because it happened yesterday, so relevance is instantly dismissed. But in the kind of discourse and debate Scotland must have about the future of the game, we shouldn't be so dismissive of what the past can teach us. This is the period in which we led at club level in European football. In terms of European countries with a population of less than 11 million people, only Sweden, out of 20 countries, qualified for more World Cup finals than Scotland. We produced some of the best – some would say *the* best – football managers in the world. We produced some of the best players in the world. We also retain world records of match attendance figures for both club and country as shown earlier in the chapter. Setting aside our dismal record of qualifying for the European Championships, this was a stunning and remarkable era in Scottish football. We should not categorise this period as merely cherished memories of a bygone era, but instead use the achievements to better understand what happened after, when the game fell off a cliff, and what we need to do to build a new and better future.

The Modern Age, The Unremarkable Age, Post-'90s

The post-'Golden Age' era provides compelling evidence of the absolute long-term decline of Scottish football. The old firm appeared in the finals of European Competitions in 2003 and 2008, attendances were reasonably steady, Celtic and Rangers reinforced their domination of the game and thankfully five clubs survived administration; Livingston, Hearts, Dunfermline, Motherwell and Dundee (twice). Gretna and Rangers entered liquidation proceedings. Gretna, after a breath-taking rise to the top, died. But Rangers, after a massive financial and board fiasco, were punished and relegated to division three, but are now back in the Premier League. This was a period of intense probing as to why neither the SFA or the SPFL had the financial and regulatory authority, or powers of due diligence, to prevent this type of crisis emerging, which had profound consequences for the rest of the game. The Rangers issue has had a serious effect on the public's confidence in football. This should have been a wake-up call and once again highlights how divorced the game is from the standards expected in the outside world. The football authorities argued that their hands were tied, that they had few powers to intervene and that this was a private business beyond the normal confines of their competence. That doesn't make sense. Football, and a club of Rangers' stature, impacts life outside Ibrox; it is an issue of Scotland-wide importance. For the good of the game, football authorities should be able to have sound procedures in place to scrutinise who runs our clubs, to enforce the financial fair play regulations of UEFA and insist on transparency and accountability.

This most recent period of the game can also be framed in the following manner. First, Scotland is a country that has massive amount of good will for the game and while that has been eroded over the last 20–30 years, there is a rich seam of passion, pride and enthusiasm to be mined. But this will not last forever, unless the game is radically transformed. Secondly, footballing DNA is present in abundance and hasn't disappeared. The importance of this point seems to be lost at the heart of the modern game, where the prevailing view is that elite talent is best left to a few clubs to find, nurture and develop. This isn't working for Scotland and makes no sense whatsoever. Third, the national game is losing out to the club game, which is in the ascendency and is distorting the distribution of finance, power, opportunity, and authority within the game. This wasn't the case in the 'Golden Age'. Scottish football is in danger of being undermined from within. The power grab may have started off as an act of narrow self-interest or self-protection, either consciously or unconsciously, for the few. But it is now fast upsetting the balance of the game and sacrificing the spirit and substance of our national team.

This shift in power between the SFA and the SPFL/SPL has been fermenting since the late '90s but has accelerated in recent years. It is currently derailing major initiatives within the game such as Project Brave – our new youth and academy policy – which has become a pale, distorted shadow of its original idea, hijacked by the few at the expense of the many. The 'Golden Age' had natural talent in abundance at a different point in the development of the world game. Elite talent was based on schools and school football. That was the key to success.

The theme for the few and not the many is undermining the membership organisation that football is supposed to represent. This wasn't the case previously. The structures of the game represent democracy in name only. The overwhelming majority of the 42 clubs have no influence in what is happening in Scottish football and the current league structure is out of step with other countries in UEFA. There is widespread acceptance in Scotland that the leagues are too small, the split in the Premier League at the end of season makes no sense and the finances of the game, and their distribution, govern the size of the Premiere league. We are not asking whether this is the best model for Scottish football. Most of the fans do not support the current structure, but because money matters and interests must be protected, there is unlikely to be any change. Most of the clubs fear using their democratic rights in the SPFL and SFA to propose change because they have become unwilling players in what is a rigged system.

No-one disputes the idea of having strong, financially-sound clubs to compete in Scotland and in Europe. No-one disputes that money and broadcasting income are now the key material influences on the game. No-one disputes the globalised nature of the game and the intense competition at European level. No-one disputes the domination of Scottish football by one club, which used to be two and could in the future be five or six. No-one disputes the fact that clubs are businesses, companies that need to keep afloat. No-one disputes the fact that clubs need a return on the financial and football capital they invest in. No-one disputes the fact that in the 'real' world, reality is knocking on the club door every day. No-one disputes the fact that clubs need to draw on the best young people.

But, all of this must never be at the expense of every other aspect of the Scottish game; or to the exclusion of our main priority, which is the success of Scotland's National side and our role on the world and European stage. It must not prevent us from ensuring that every part of Scotland plays its part in finding, nurturing and developing the best football talent or ensuring that a membership organisation does not operate in name only, where the few dictate to the many. It must not stop the game from having a bigger ambition than merely the sum of a few big clubs or exclude the idea that the current structure of governance is not fit for purpose and is the main reason why the game is in decline. Part of the club game is in the ascendency but the rest of the game, especially the SFA, is in decline, stripped of authority and being the subject of a silent but obvious coup at the heart of the game.

The performance of Scottish clubs in Europe even with the benefits of the 'power grab' has been uninspiring, with our coefficients and ability to qualify worsening from the '90s onwards. So even when helped by a large injection of finance, success has been elusive, two clubs have dominated and while Scotland can boast of having the highest per-capita football attendances of all the nations within UEFA, which is significant but slightly distorted by the massive attendances of two great clubs, has the overall quality of our club game improved?

There are many immediate threats to Scottish football in the post-'Golden Age' era, but three stand out. This may seem harsh and uncompromising but they are clear from the evidence available.

The first is that the governance of the game is not fit for purpose and there is compelling evidence to suggest that the institution, its culture, its structures, the vision, the ambition and links with the world outside football are all in urgent need of renewal.

The second threat is the intended or unintended insurgency by the clubs, into the wider game, and in particular, the preserve of the SFA and the 'hijacking' of youth policy which made matters much worse and has to be challenged. It is in the long-term interests of the wider club membership and the common good of football that there be a rebalancing of intent, power, finance, authority and resources within the game.

Third, an obvious, but important point to make is the narrowing down of the game, and the question of whose interests are being served; the amount of broadcasting and media time given over to Rangers and Celtic is both understandable and ludicrous. Papers need readers. These are clubs with large numbers of supporters. They make news and are often controversial. The clubs raise issues of importance to Scottish society as a whole, that will be newsworthy. This is good copy but they are only a part of the game, and whilst acres of newsprint are turned over to the Old Firm, what about the wider game. Arguing for the wider common good of the game does require a broader coverage of what is going on in Scottish football.

The decline of the game in Scotland is NOT an act of nature, like the eclipse of the moon or the earth orbiting the sun. It was made in Scotland. Since the mid-80s we have collectively failed to understand and adapt to the changing scene of world football; the new hungry enthusiastic aspirational teams on the block, the massive changes in society, the new politics of Scotland, the transfer of nationalism from the back of a Scottish jersey to other political struggles and the myriad of changes within the game itself. This would be a monumental set of 21st century challenges for any type of organisation to face, but our dilemma was severely worsened by an institution that was shaped in the 20th century and burdened by the legacy of a previous era; self-interest and protecting the status quo are powerful inhibitors. It is hard to acknowledge that we are not good enough and do something about it. It is easier to muddle through and ignore the real world.

The Old and The New

Bringing together the soul of Scotland's past with the spirit of Scotland's football future is an important way of confirming my belief that there is a bright future for Scottish football, one that can be created around a unity of purpose, shared belief, and a passion for what is more than a game. The new Scotland, modern and confident, needs a game that will match its aspirations, be comfortable with breaking new ground and be willing to seek success in different ways that were never even dreamed about a century ago.

Before looking in detail at why the game fell over a cliff and how we got to where we are, let's consider this quote from *What has Scottish football ever done for us?* by Greg Johnson.

> Jock Stein's immortal European Cup triumph with a Celtic team of local Glaswegians still stands as a unique achievement in European football and a high water mark in the Scottish game. It shouldn't be suggested that such feats may be achievable any time soon, but there is also no reason why such talent no longer exists or why managers can't innovate tactically to create a team greater than the sum of its parts. Celtic's Lisbon Lions smashed the invincible cynicism of Catenaccio with beautiful, fluid attacking football-intelligent, youthful players switching positions and pulling the Italians to pieces with unpredictable plays. Steins overlapping fullbacks traded places with forwards in a game plan that pre-empted Total Football, with a style, years ahead of its time.

The history of Scottish football from the inception of the SFA in 1873 will mean different things to different people. But for most of us, it is about passion, pride and a shared sense of how important the game is to the nation. Despite setbacks in our international and club history, we must remain committed to big ambitions and a determination to succeed. Perhaps this is a good time to reflect, as the memories of the past fade and we move through the to new dreams of the future. There is a new generation of potential fans out there. We do live in a very different world. So, what is it we want to achieve? But first, how did we get here?

CHAPTER SEVEN

A Game in Decline: How did we get here?

MANY ATTEMPTS HAVE BEEN made to explain why the 'Golden Age' of Scottish football in the '60s, '70s, and '80s gave way, so suddenly and dramatically, to a period of decline. There is an endless debate on whether there is a better future ahead or whether we are condemned to a modest club game existence with limited domestic high points; where international success for club and country remains in our consciousness as memories, but not as dreams.

Coverage of our decline has provided some startling headlines. 'SOS Scotland: Is there a way back for a once great footballing nation?' or 'Scottish football's pathetic TV deal is bottom of the Euro Table'. 'Scottish football's crisis of confidence', 'Pitches, coaches and iPads; what are the reasons for Scotland's talent decline', 'What is happening to Scottish football?' and 'The decline of Scotland as an international football team'. The coverage over decades has been seeking answers to some searching questions, many of them expressing the disappointment and frustration of our incredible and long-suffering fans, and all of them desperate to find the philosopher's stone or the magical elixir that could return the game to its former glory days.

This chapter takes up the challenge of why the game declined and asks the simple question: why, after a generation of a feast of football, did the game fall off a cliff in the mid-90s and bring in the years of football famine? I make no apologies for the drama of the question. There is a story to be told which could help us shape a different future. One which acknowledges the importance and complexity of the social, economic, lifestyle and political changes that are impacting football and our lives generally, and which are so difficult to comprehend and deal with. But a story that also believes that Scottish football has a bigger future but one where the path to progress must be defined by the brutal facts of reality, which the game currently is either unable or unwilling to face up to.

A Sidebar of Significance

Reinforcing my sense of optimism are the findings of the 'Fan Attendance Report', commissioned by the European Professional Football League and published in January 2018. The organisation, representing 32 leagues in 25 countries, measured attendances at matches over the seven seasons, from 2010 to 2016. Patrick McPartlin, writing in the Scotsman said:

> Among the findings were that the English Premiere League had the highest cumulative attendances in Europe and the English Football League saw the highest gates out with Europe's top tiers. But the Scottish Premiership leads the way throughout Europe on a per capita basis.

In terms of the average gates per game, the Scottish Premiership is ranked number seven. But Scotland out performs Germany, England, Spain, Italy, and France when the country's relative population is factored in. In contrast to other parts of the game, the Scottish Premiership is punching above its weight in per-capita attendance figures. The top flight in Scotland – only one part of a much broader game – is holding on to its base, despite the overall decline of the game. This is double edged. While it encourages attendance figures, there is also a cost to the rest of the SPFL and other aspects of the game? To what extent does this reflect the overall health of the league structure?

Understanding Change

Change is complex, threatening and difficult to deal with and throughout history has determined the fate of empires, countries, and an infinite variety of institutions, both large and small. Scottish football is no different. We now have a better idea of what success meant in the 'Golden Age', but looking ahead over the next 20 years, what will success look like? To answer that question, we need to assess how we got here, and why and when that decline began.

The long history of the game for which Scotland was an early starter, the second association to be formed worldwide and, as a result, developed a rules-based game which helped establish a strong foundation upon which to build, and then led to the setting up of the SFA and the Scottish league before the end of the 19th century.

Then we must consider the pre-war, inter-war and post-war period. Clubs were formed, a strong league structure was established, the competition was fierce, and the ideas of community, solidarity and club loyalty reflected the sense of identity and class-consciousness of a passionate fan base. Clubs, who have now slipped from public view, had remarkable successes.

We must acknowledge that a "Golden Age" of consolidation, incredible success in Scotland, Europe and on the international stage, showed remarkable achievements. But also the last 30 years, where we exited the higher levels of the international game, failed to win in Europe and where two clubs dominated the club game. A period where the shape of the leagues became more reflective of the distribution of power and finance within the game and less about the wider needs of the game and common sense. From its earliest beginnings, Scotland was moving positively forward for just over a century, then we stopped, reshaped our game around a few clubs, lowered our level of ambition and settled into a modest and much less challenging regime of domestic football.

Was there a 'big bang' where some seismic event knocked us off course and put us into a different orbit from our previous football history, the aspirations of fans and the needs of a rapidly modernising Scotland? Or was our future determined by a series of events, issues and influences that may pass unnoticed at the time but cumulatively have taken their toll on the game? What was happening in Scottish society that led to Scots loosening their emotional grip on a game that had been so influential in their lives? Were sport and football becoming less important? What specific changes were taking place within the game itself that could have had such an impact on our ambitions, and the nationalism and patriotism that were so inextricably linked to football? Was the 'Golden Age' just a piece of luck where the constellation of the stars was in perfect alignment, never to be repeated?

Was it the case that the burden of history and a legacy of institutional inertia had created football authorities that were singularly ill equipped to either understand change or deal with its consequences and were driven into an insular and defensive posture, which elevated protection above innovation and inspiration? It could be considered that some saw the decline of the game as an opportunity to organise a 'power grab', change the face of Scottish football and create a game in which the interests of a few clubs would dominate based on eventually changing, long-term established priorities spurred on by a new financial regime. If this is so, was there a reasonable case for the few to eventually oversee the many, or did this merely exacerbate the immediate post 'Golden Age' challenges of the game and result –consciously or unconsciously – in unintended consequences that are proving so hugely damaging to a broader, common good approach to Scottish football?

The psychology of the game is important. When priorities change, by intent or accident, the whole dynamic of effort and outcomes is altered. The new becomes the normal and people then become unaware of the cumulative damage it is causing. What may have started off as a way of safeguarding the interests of a few and the integrity of the top league in Scottish football, has rapidly eaten away at the fabric of football and taken us on an extremely limited journey within a comfort zone where a contented minority have exclusive authority. Confronting facts becomes difficult as the wagons circle and the inner space gets smaller. This is the difference between the opportunity to, 'have your say' and the opportunity to be heard. Scotland has been talking to the game for some time, but few people are listening. We need to rip away so much of the noise and clutter surrounding the game and start to focus on the few things that will have the greatest impact as we collectively try to modernise and return Scottish football to its rightful place, in a Scotland that is moving rapidly forward, on all fronts.

The Decline of the Game

In a brilliant series of four documentaries, *Scotland's Game*, BBC Scotland produced, in 2016, an attempt to understand the current state of football and how it had arrived. Part of the summary of this output was the publication of '11 Surprising facts that show how Scottish football has changed over the last 30 years'. They are listed here as a good starting point for my analysis.

'11 Surprising facts that show how Scottish football has changed over the last 30 years'   BBC, 2016

1. The 1987 Scottish Cup Final, when St Mirren beat Dundee United, was the last time when all of the players, managers and officials were all Scots.

2. The league match between Celtic and Rangers on 4 October 2003 featured only one Scottish player in the two starting line ups: Jackie McNamara, Maurice Ross came on as substitutes for Rangers, Celtic won 1-0.

3. In 1986, as the Scotland national team was heading to the world cup in Mexico, 97% of the players playing in the top Scottish league were born in Scotland. At the start of the 2015/6 season, only 54% of the top league players were born in Scotland.

4. At the start of the 2016/6 season, Ross County, St Johnstone and Dundee had the most Scots-born players in their teams, with 73% each. Inverness Caledonian Thistle had the lowest number of Scots-born players at 7%. The majority of Caley's squad were born in England.

5. Of all the players who started the first match of the 2015/6 Scottish Premiere season, 77% were born in the United Kingdom and 35% were born in England.

6. During the Scottish Premier league era from 1998-2013, five clubs survived administration: Livingston, Hearts, Dunfermline, Motherwell and Dundee (twice). Two entered liquidation proceedings: Gretna and Rangers FC.

7. According to the SPFL, more people per head of the population attend football matches in Scotland than any other country in Europe.

8. Only two Scottish players have won the Champions league: Paul Lambert and Darren Fletcher.

9. The last club to win Scotland's top-flight league title – other than Celtic or Rangers – was Aberdeen in 1985, over 31 years ago.

10. Scotland have not qualified for a major international tournament since 1998 – the same year that the two-pound coin was first issued, DVDs became available in the UK and Britain last hosted the Eurovision Song Contest.

11. Theo Snelders was the first non-Scot to win the PFA Scotland player of the year award in 1989 while at Aberdeen. In the 27 years since his win, only 10 scots have won the award, and only two non-Old Firm players have won it.

Against this background, three developments stand out. First, the game had rapidly changed between the mid-80s and the present time, and the number of Scots playing in the top league had declined. Second, the number of foreign players had increased dramatically and third, fewer Scots and more foreign players meant diminishing opportunities for young Scots.

First Order Issues

The creation of the SPL, now the Scottish Premiership, has had a seismic impact on Scottish football and represents, paradoxically, one of the primary reasons for the decline of the wider game. The new era of broadcasting has brought with it many benefits for the viewing public but has undermined the importance and influence of the fan-base. The new finances of the top league have become worshipped as an all powerful solution to the problems of the game, a powerful brake on any further league reforms and a source of further division as the distribution of power, money and authority creates a chasm between the few and the many. The power of money, broadcasting income, short-term thinking, protectionism and the consequences of the 'power grab', act as a powerful block to reform and could eventually destroy the unity of purpose and the credibility of an integrated game, which the majority of fans want to see. A strong and vibrant club game is essential. No one disputes that. But not at the expense of youth talent, the remainder of Scottish clubs or the national team; that would be a price too far.

The forces that have been unleashed by these changes may not win success in the longer term, but in the mean time could also alienate much of the game in the process. The struggle, which is emerging, between the SFA and the SPFL – club versus country – is the most obvious and telling feature of the internal conflicts of the game. BBC Scotland in *Scotland's Game* described their programme,

> ...as a look at the last three decades of intrigue, social change,
> greed risk and self- delusion, charting the gradual demise against
> a backdrop of rapid social change.

The player profile of the Scottish Premiership has changed, and I would argue that this has a helped create a crisis in finding and developing young talent. The conveyor belt of bright and talented young Scots became the victim of the short-term idea of 'the finished product'. Young talent Scots have become too much of an effort and we run the risk of not only damaging our clubs but also our prospects on the international stage. Young people and their undoubted talents are the life-blood of Scottish football, past and present. In the 'Golden Age' of the game, theirs was an array of young talent. It was natural, abundant, and appreciated as the wealth of the game, our human capital as a footballing nation.

In this, the schools were crucial. Margaret Thatcher's teacher's strike in 1985 dealt a cruel blow to the game and changed everything. Alex Ferguson has made wise and powerful claims to the idea that the demise of school's football accelerated the decline of Scottish football. Thousands of dedicated teachers who had used their private time to teach youngsters were disillusioned and, as a result, the schools as the main suppliers of talent just ceased to be a force. To date there has been no adequate alternative and despite the good work by the SFA, the league clubs, the extensive network of clubs comprising the wider national game and the development of a new youth strategy, the conveyor belt of elite talent is not yet back in business. But it could be.

In addition to the negative impact of what I would regard as 'first order' issues explaining the decline of the game, there are many other factors that have added to the grim analysis of the current situation and how we got here. Graham Spiers, in a perceptive, sometimes sentimental, but always illuminating piece in *The Herald* in 2012, charts Scotland's downfall on the global stage and suggests six reasons to explain it.

> The death of street football, a modern necessity, killed off the 'natural womb' of talent the country once had. Scottish kids once played fitba' till the dying of the light. No more.
>
> Scottish society improved, social conditions were enhanced, and the urchin-footballer went with it. Social deprivation was once a prolific conveyor of gifted players. No more.
>
> The Scottish FA endured decades of neglect. While other countries – the Scandinavians – were putting coaching structures in place, the Scottish FA said: 'We're alright, we're going to all these World Cups. What a price Scotland has paid.
>
> The Modern 'idle age' means kids no longer go out to play. At one time you put a jumper down in a park. In recent times you'd open a computer screen while scoffing Monster Munchies.
>
> Rangers and Celtic in part killed the 'grow your own' culture of Scottish football by spending two decades buying in

'big names'. Other SPL clubs scrambled to keep pace. Patience in rearing young Scots went by the wayside.

Football used to dominate school sports –in part unfairly. Today other sports have muscled in on the agenda. Educationally, Scotland has ceased to be a football-orientated country.

This analysis is understandably strengthened by emotion, which adds credibility to the comments. The past-times of modern children and young people are, however, mirrored in other countries. Poverty has never been a driving force in Sweden and Denmark who qualify for international tournaments regularly, and in Iceland, who have exploded recently onto the international scene. I am sure that cars have killed off street football everywhere. His references to the impact of Rangers and Celtic on our game, the failure to retain a high profile for football in schools and the performance of our youth strategy all have salience and provide further evidence of football authorities in Scotland falling behind old and new international competitors.

The Politics of Scotland

The politics of Scotland have changed beyond recognition in the devolution years. There is little doubt that between the Scotland Act 1998 and the independence referendum in 2014, the new Scotland is more conscious of identity and more confident in what it does. A great deal of nationalism and patriotism has shifted from football to politics. As Scotland's appearances on the international football stage have diminished, the importance of post-devolution politics has intensified. There are now many more forums for Scottishness to be expressed. The nation has travelled far since the Scotland versus England struggles, where every game was a re-run of Bannockburn. Scotland now has its own parliament, which represents another reference point for the spirit, soul, and psyche of Scotland to be expressed. Nationalism has moved from the back of a blue football jersey to tea shirts, banners, political rallies and mass-marketing.

Jock Stein

The death of Jock Stein is often referenced as an important turning point in Scottish football. As a giant of the game and the most successful manager in Scottish football history, his collapse at the end of the World Cup qualifying match shook this country to its foundations. The iconic superstar was seen as more than just a football manager and would go down in history along- side Busby, Ferguson and Shankly as national heroes, at a time when both the country and the game needed them. Football is a very spiritual and sentimental part of our national life, and especially at that time. I have no doubts that the death of Jock stein on 10 September 1985 was a defining moment as the 'Golden Age' football was about to transition into a lesser period of success for Scotland.

Bosman and Sky

Bosman and Sky had a huge influence on the game. The Bosman ruling succeeded in abolishing quotas on foreign players and gave all EU players the right to a free transfer at the end of their contracts. Bosman, a 1995 European Court of Justice ruling, also coincided with an explosion of TV broadcasting revenues. Sky deals were concluded in Scotland, but at only a fraction of the English Premier League. This, together with Bosman, initially had a significant and detrimental effect on club finance, but the more serious and long-term consequence was the massive influx of foreign players into the Scottish game.

It is worth pausing at this point to recognise the extraordinary financial difficulties that the new SPL was getting into, early in the new century. This may be one of the reasons why the now named Scottish Premiership is so protective of its income, and so keen to exert a tighter grip on all aspects of the game, distorting further the already unequal distribution of income their way. This means that future league reforms could be blocked, not in terms of 'good for the game' criteria, but to enable significant financial interests to be protected. This doesn't make much sense.

But going back to the early years of this new millennium, this turbulent period of attracting broadcasting money and Bosman brought pressures on wage bills, profitability, and debt levels. A Price Water House Cooper report suggested that a benchmark sustainable wage-to-turnover ratio for football clubs should be 60%. In 2001–2, only Celtic was below this benchmark at 58%. The report also confirmed that five of the top 12 clubs were technically insolvent and their liabilities exceeded their assets.

Another factor contributing to the financial problem was the collapse of the SPL's deal with Sky. Following this, Motherwell, Dundee and Livingston went into administration between 2002 and 2004. In 2008, Gretna became the fourth club to go into administration. The cumulative debts of the SPL reached a climax in in 2003, attaining a level of £185.9 million. The prospect of further clubs entering administration combined with unprecedented and unsustainable debt levels acted as a catalyst for change. To illustrate the fears of the top league, their pre-occupation with protectionism and their obsession with how the football cake is divided, it is important to remind ourselves of what a crisis looks like, 'From 1989 to 2001 the combined wages of the SPL increased by an incredible 957% from £10.5 million to £110 million!' We do have a game where money dominates, but is there a point at which the needs of the whole game become much bigger than the needs of the few, and different choices must be made.

Rangers football club entered administration in February 2012. This was one of the low points of Scottish football history and the start of a chaotic and deeply worrying process of saving a once great football team and ensuring that a club that was too big to fail, returned to the Scottish premiership in a better financial state, and with radically improved governance fit for the 21st century. This raises the question of how powerful businesses can be properly regulated and controlled by the football authorities in the interests of the fans, players, communities, and country. This clearly didn't happen with Rangers. This is an important issue for football fans. Club fans, with few exceptions, do not have any real or effective controls over how clubs are run, any say in matters of Board membership or oversight of who's trust is being invested in to take care of historical and community assets, that may have existed for decades. Rangers fans, frustrated at this heart-breaking experience, could only scream and shout from the side-lines as their iconic and beloved team were being dragged down by people they barely knew, but whom they had to trust with their most important asset. Scotland has a poor record of fan involvement despite the efforts of fan organisations. Unlike Germany, where there is a much more open and inclusive approach to fans, Scotland has only moved very slowly towards fan involvement, community ownership and board participation. What is taken as common-place in Europe is seen as unnecessary here. This is another area that is holding Scottish football back. At times like this, when the game is in decline and there is much fan disquiet, anger and resentment, there should be a serious attempt to involve fans and enhance their role in improving the game. Once again, Scotland is out of step with other countries.

The League Structure

In its first seasons, the Scottish Football League had 11 clubs, with a second division introduced in 1893. Until 1922, promotion was based on a ballot of clubs rather than sporting merit. Before the 1975–6 season, the Scottish Football League had a divisional structure with two divisions. A three-tier league structure was introduced in 1975, with the introduction of a ten club Premier division. Between 1975–6 and 1994, Scotland had a three divisional structure. Then from season 1994–5, a four-division structure was introduced, including a new third division and with all divisions compromising of ten clubs. Until 1997, there was only one league structure in Scotland. The next major change took place in 1998 when the Premier League clubs split from the Scottish Football League to establish the SPL. Further changes have taken place in the last few years, including the setting up of the Scottish Professional Football League in June 2013, the demise of the Scottish Football League, the renaming of the SPL as the Scottish Premiership, the development of a pyramid system, the regionalisation of the leagues outside the SPFL and more competitive game deciders. There are presently 12 clubs in the SPL and a further 30 in the three other divisions of the SPFL.

Post-1998, the debate on the future structure of the leagues has continued. Originally the SPL contained ten clubs, but it was subsequently enlarged to 12 for the 2000–1 season. Since then, the SPL has operated, 'a split league format' to prevent the need for a 44-game schedule, which was once used in the Scottish Premier division. The issue of finance now dominates the debate. Many Scottish fans do not support our nearly unique league structure, the split format or the size of the leagues, and would like to see a further discussion on reconstruction.

This is unlikely to happen because the power is out of their hands and financial issues prevent new thinking about growing the game and creating larger leagues. In the post-'Golden Age', money is in danger of distorting the football debate. Even worse, it increases the drive of the Scottish Premiership to protect their interests by seeing policy areas, such as our youth strategy, as less about investment in young talent and more about income for clubs. The lack of effective democracy within the SPFL, a membership organisation in name only, means that safeguards are weak and opportunities for change are rare, unless there is a massive shake up in how the SFA, SP and SPFL are run. Once a structure becomes a vehicle for safe-guards and self-interest, the game's future can start to unravel.

How We Got Here

Scotland has changed and so has the beautiful game.

Phase one was the failure to understand what was happening. The practical consequences of decline, evident after the mid-90s, appeared later than the events and issues which had caused them. My argument is based on the notion that the changes to the game, cumulative in effect and diverse in nature, were never recognised or understood by the football authorities. They never had any reason to believe that change was impacting the game. They had no collective capacity to be analytical or reflective, if that was needed. And, like many organisations throughout history, they were institutionally and culturally unable to see the game through the prism of a changing Scotland, a globalising world and changing expectations.

Phase two accelerated the decline post-1998 when despite the evidence piling up with clubs making little progress in European competitions – Rangers and Celtic being the exception by making it to two Euro finals – and failing to qualify for either the World cup or the European championships, there was still hardly any real acceptance that a crisis was in the making. It was business as usual.

Phase three got underway when the Scottish Premier League, emerged and changed the whole dynamic of Scottish football. Instead of being an event to modernise or rejuvenate the game, it became an opportunity for the few to lead the many and start to build this elaborate fortress into which few would be invited in, but that would leave many outside meaning that much of the football effort would be narrowed and focussed on self-interest and protection.

Phase four overlaps with three and reveals a period where the SPL, clubs and finance take centre stage as the game lurches from one financial issue to another in the first decade of the new millennium. Sadly, this ensures that important issues such as youth policy, football facilities, international competition, the national team, and the developing women's game are side-lined and the whole momentum of the game slackens. The nation and the fans then become disillusioned and Scotland starts to take amore critical view of its favourite sport.

Phase five starts with Gordon Smith CE of the SFA and his Chair, George Peat, the President of the SFA, asking me in 2009–10 to undertake a review of the game, which I was genuinely honoured and delighted to carry out. Based on my recommendations contained in two reports, the SFA embarked on a period in which some of the big and urgent policy issues of governance, youth policy and institutional change would figure prominently, as well as other issues that needed a public airing after being off the agenda since the '80s and certainly off the agenda in the period after the SPL was in place.

Phase six started with great expectations. For nearly a decade progress has been made on a number of fronts since the publication of my review. But momentum has slackened, priorities are being contested, limited institutional change has taken place, the youth strategy seems to have been waylaid, the SFA is still under attack and is in less good shape than it should be and the 'circling of the waggons' approach to the outside world has been strengthened. This is not where we should be a generation after the 'Golden Age' and 20 years since we fell off the cliff, and nearly a decade after my own review.

Phase seven overlaps with phases five and six, and illustrates the growing disconnect between the game and the changing nature of Scottish society: a period in which further modernisation was needed but was held back because of the insularity of the football authorities and their failure to do what Scotland expected of them. An institutional attitude of mind meant the game didn't engage with new and emerging issues and this added to public perceptions that the game was becoming remote from new ideas that were both relevant for football and for their lives. Lagging behind on live social issues reinforced the decline of the game and generally added to the increasingly held view that football was becoming more detached. As public, fans and government became more frustrated and let down, the game appeared resentful of 'interference' and, at times, seemed irritated by the notion that problems of society should be linked to football. By failing to respond to the challenges of society, the game is added to its decline.

The most obvious example was the women's game, part of Scottish life for a very long time but only recognised, here and internationally, over the last two decades for its true worth. Meeting with the Scottish women's coach in 2010, I was struck by the passion, professionalism and the seriousness attached to their desire to be a serious part of modern football. Over the past few years, tremendous progress has been made. A game totally dominated by men has been slow to appreciate the achievements of the women's game and the vast potential of what is on offer. Qualifying for the European Championships was a big step. They are now doing well in the group for the next women's World Cup and have a great chance of qualifying for the finals. But the potential goes well beyond this. It is likely to be the fastest growing part of the game. Getting girls and young women involved is a great boost to fitness, health and wellbeing and chimes well with the aspirations of government to improve the health of the nation and tackle such issues as obesity. There is no doubting the potential for the women's game in Scotland to be a force world-wide. For this to happen, the game must respect diversity, equality and rid itself of the notions of the past. In the darker recesses of the game, there lurks some primitive views about the role of women in football, including the idea that a women's place is not on the pitch, and this in itself is a definition of decline. As life moves on, so should Scottish football.

Modern Times

There are of course a huge number of other issues which figure prominently in the national football debate but are, by their very nature, also core concerns of a wider modern society. Sadly, many of these issues that transcend the boundaries of football and society, illustrate the growing divide between what the game thinks is acceptable and what the public expects. The list is long, but not exhaustive;

- The lack of serious fan involvement in the running of the game.

- A narrowing of the fan base with little evidence of the game reaching out to encourage a more diversified audience.

- Expanding the fan experience through improved in-ground facilities and recognising that the game should be about entertainment, which carries with it a sense that there are new customers and consumers to be attracted to the game; like comparing a visit to a modern Odeon cinema complex today with a visit to my old cinema 50 years ago – The Imperial in Methil. Significant progress has been made, but there is along way to go.

- Steps to improve the oversight of clubs, including issues of regulation, ethics, due diligence, financial probity and 'fit and proper' people assessments.

- The potential for a football ombudsman.

- Relationships with other sports, which are very limited.

- Views on anti-social behaviour, differences between government and the game on how to tackle sectarianism and bigotry, and the reality of competing religious views and cultures. Is this an issue for club or country and who is responsible?

- Sponsorship and the excessive contribution from betting firms. A controversial issue in society is the mainstay of the Scottish game. The English FA has agreed to phase it out. Tobacco was big in sport, but no longer. Alcohol used to dominate football, but no longer. Should betting be next? There is a direct conflict of interest in addition to the ethical and addiction concerns. If football was more mainstream, successful, and more connected, it could attract more attention and finance: government has to be careful about what it invests in.

- Protections for children and young people in the game; the concerns of the Children's Commissioner in Scotland, the issue of child sex abuse and the problems surrounding the contractual relationships between youth players and professional clubs.

- Health and care issues, such as dementia, where a great deal of news coverage has, understandably, focussed on former football players with the condition. The National Football League (NFL) in the United States has been active and initiated safeguards for school age children playing the game. How far should the responsibilities of football reach?

These are important issues for football and society, but the game is less connected than it should be. Football is by far the most important sport in Scotland and could make a much bigger contribution to national life. But for a variety of reasons, it is holding itself back. As the game has declined and the focus has narrowed, footballs contribution to the wider good of Scotland has also diminished. We are only adding to the perception that football is out of step with what our country is trying to achieve. When modernity demands more, we look out of place. Phase seven is the next phase of the Scottish football story. What might that involve? What could success look like? How can it be delivered? In the coming chapters, I will set out what I think it might look like and how this renaissance can be achieved!

CHAPTER EIGHT

What Happened to the Review of 2010?

I WAS ABSOLUTELY DELIGHTED and privileged, to be asked by the SFA in 2009, to undertake a major 'Review of Scottish Football', covering the development of Scotland's young talent and the future of the SFA. Two reports were published in 2010 and the recommendations were overwhelmingly implemented. The first report dealt with, 'The Grassroots, Recreation and Youth Development', and the second report addressed 'Governance, Leadership and Structures'. Hampden, home of the SFA, SPL and the Scottish Football League, which would disappear as part of the merger in 2013 when the SPFL was established, was at a low point. The publication of the findings and recommendations was seen by many as an important but one-time occurrence. There was no suggestion at the time that this process of review, reform and renewal would become a permanent feature of the game. A vigorous process commenced but has since stalled. While key areas of policy, important areas of governance, and an overall strategy for youth development were tackled, the big issues of culture, institutions, and structures and the more complex issues of ambition, strategy, vision and principles were not really high on the agenda or list of things to do. The practical tasks were more immediate, especially the youth strategy.

Looking at the review of 2010 allows me to reflect on the positive outcomes but also to identify the shortcomings and mourn the fact that a comprehensive and far-reaching strategy to boost youth talent has faltered. It appears now to be the victim or a consequence of the 'power grab', the declining authority of the SFA and the narrowing of an ambition, which was designed to create a world-class model for youth policy. A unique opportunity, based on a great deal of good will and top-class expertise and experience, is in danger of being squandered. This is of crucial significance. Scotland needs talented young players.

The first part of the review had three objectives. First, to provide an extensive review of grassroots football and youth development linked to an examination of facilities and resources currently available for the development of young players. Second, was to undertake a critical analysis of the way in which young talent is identified, nurtured and developed, and to look at the experience of other countries. The third objective was to look at the interface between the grassroots, recreation and youth development and the professional club game, and in this context, the relationships between the football authorities. My growing sense of disappointment is heightened by the fact that this part of the review was based on a comprehensive dialogue reflecting the widest possible range of football interests consulted.

A Great Opportunity

At a time of considerable stress and low morale at Hampden, this was inevitably a review that would embrace change based on the art of the possible and not be seen as an opportunity to be so futuristic or adventurous that the faithful would react adversely and undermine the prospect of any of the reforms going ahead. Football politics are immensely complex. The game had a long history with well-established procedures, traditions and deeply entrenched views that did not easily bend towards radical change. There were obvious strains and tensions between the SFA and the two league organisations as well as a real sense of club ascendency and a weakening of the authority of the SFA. What struck me initially was the lack of overall direction to the total game and the fact that club structure and national game had an uneasy relationship. But when we talk now of the 'game', as I have done through out the book, there really isn't one. Football is a collection of different games, ideas, concepts, processes and structures that are not currently united around a set of historic ideals or ideas. The unity of previous eras, no longer exists.

So, I was always conscious of the need to balance one side against the other. This is not to undermine the sense of commitment of anyone involved but it was hard to work out what degree of reform would be acceptable and workable, and what could reasonably be left to another day. Significantly for me, the SFA's authority and influence have diminished further over the last eight years. More disconcerting is my impression that, by accident or design, the work of the SFA has been downgraded. This is not the reform I was seeking but with different institutions in the mix, the power and finance of the SPL, and the ineffective, membership structure of the club game, this was probably inevitable.

If I Only Knew Then...

Writing this chapter leads me to think of the idea, 'if I knew then what I know now', what a different set of findings and recommendations would have emerged. I totally underestimated the impact of legacy, the state of organisations that were not equipped for the challenges of the modern era, the severe cultural constraints, institutional inertia, the depth of insecurity and the evidence of the power grab that was underway at this time. The SPL was anxious about its problems but quietly confident about its largely unstated direction of travel. The Hampden HQ was in a much worse state that I had imagined. Short-termism was everywhere, but it was not seen as a problem because the organisations worked for the moment and were absorbed in often frenetic and protracted skirmishes with the outside world over a variety of issues. But I liked the personalities and their interest in the game. They were pragmatists not idealists, professionals not pundits, cautious and concerned and, at the time of the review, anxious about the future of football.

This was the problem; there was no big picture, no yellow brick road, no vision or big ambition for the game in total, there were only bits of that in relation to bits of the game. My impression looking back to the time of the review was of a game that was removed from its history, strangely detached and disconnected from life outside the game. It was unconnected to a Scotland that still pined for progress, it didn't understand how much football meant to most communities or the thousands of clubs that existed and it didn't welcome the interference or intrusion by media, government and critical friends who were often labelled as critical enemies.

Part of the review looked at the question of league reconstruction but this was very much supplementary to the extensive work that the SPL had already been doing. This was where I experienced the gulf that existed between the SPL, as it was then, and the fans. The current league structure, as we discussed earlier, is now a prisoner of the delicate financial structure of the club game and the prospects of change seem remote. Out of step with other European countries, the league setup screams out for reform. This is a view shared by the fans, but they have no say. I find it hard to figure out why people who are fans, financiers, consumers, customers, helpers, advocates, cheerleaders and much more, are treated with such disdain and have little or no say in what happens to **their** game. Unbelievably passionate and proud people are locked out of the history, reality, and future they helped create.

Their dilemma is likely to continue as the league structure and its compliant, undemocratic membership structure is not able or willing to let them in. The fans themselves are not east to organise and the disparate nature of the fan-base is not easy to overcome, but we can surely do better.

This is where the idea of a Football Ombudsman, or maybe government intervention, are worthy of consideration based on my firmly-held view that the future of football is too important to be left to the game. The idea that fans must have a bigger say was included in my review, but as yet, no progress has been made. To make matters worse we have two supporters' organisations in Scotland and to make the fans' case more attractive and convincing, one organisation would make sense. It is worth looking at my review in a bit more detail; some extracts from the reports show a hard-hitting assessment of the game and the need for change.

Extract from 'Review of Scottish Football'

2010, details...

Tough Analysis

There is no obvious or easy solution to the many challenges facing football. Problems of lack of finance, a fear of failure, a future of uncertainty, a slowly declining fan base and a continuing focus on the weaknesses of the game are all creating extraordinary pressures on Chairs and Boards of every club. This is understandable as we acknowledge the competitive nature of club football. We have to embrace the world outside football. We are inclusive and have a sense of how important external issues are to our game.

We need to bring the game into the 21st century. Some progress has been made but there is an enormous amount of work still to be done. The issue of why the game remains stuck in the past and years away from being family friendly and being serious about attracting more woman, children and young people to our games. Football is a sport not a cause, not a celebration of battles won or lost in the mists of time and history and which have little relevance for the world we live in. Sentiment and football history are important part of our club traditions but the game is in danger of projecting an image of intolerance, negativity, lack of trust and respect, little goodwill, and in some cases a near poisonous atmosphere, which does the game no end of harm. This should have no place in our football.

Modernity has no place for this. Some cynics might suggest that this is an essential part of our game which brings excitement and solidarity and creates more interests for the Broadcasters! Whether any of that is true, one thing is clear it is not increasing attendances at games or winning new sponsors or investors. Overall the game is not attractive, but it could be. This is our challenge but the revolution in attitude has to come from the top. We need to build on the remarkable history and achievement of our club game over the last 100 years and the memories and high points of a nation that until recently has punched above its weight in World and European football.

In football we want rivalry not hatred. We want competitive games and entertaining football. We want tolerance and respect. At a time when Scottish football is facing so many challenges we don't need any distractions. The great traditions, history and goodwill our clubs have built up play a great part of the sentiment and substance that surrounds our love for the game. That is why it is in every-one's interest to make football as attractive as possible. Twenty or thirty years from now, what memories will we have of today's game? We do have to see ourselves as others see us...

We need a better understanding of the future and the dramatic changes, which are going to transform sport, leisure, health, well-being and football. We are incredibly slow about the whole "change agenda". There is no god given reason that children or young people will want to play football in the future with so many alternative attractions available to them. We need to have a better understanding of the future and the trends that are likely to influence it.

Do we continue to see football slide more and more towards a narrowing core support with all the implications that will have for the game OR do we have a vision of football as part of a modern competitive sports-based leisure and entertainment concept where children, young people, men and women, families watch competitive quality football as a pleasurable social and sporting activity but in a totally inspiring and comfortable environment? The answer is obvious. But how many see the future of the game like this. We need start to plan for it now. Other countries are already doing this.

Improving quality and the long term attractiveness of the game can only be secured through a total commitment to the development of elite talented young people Acknowledging commercial pressures and the competitive nature of the game, we have to do more now to accelerate progress towards this goal. That means that thinking Scottish, playing Scottish, investing in Scottish becomes the default positions. This will help make a bigger contribution to the national game than currently is the case.

The public are very supportive of this. Of course, there are huge pressures on every club, every week to win and be successful as both businesses facing difficult times and the fact that the energies and resources of the clubs have to be focussed on the day to day problems and issues as they appear. In this situation it is difficult to see the proverbial wood from the trees, think beyond the club level and acknowledge that there is a formidable set of opportunities and threats that require a new urgency and a renewed sense of collective endeavour and unity of purpose. This in turn demands new thinking and a new framework within which we address change and build a new future."

Setting the Scene

Overall football in Scotland is in a fragile condition. A fear of finance and fear of failure are all too evident in the fabric of our game. Once again this is leading to a search for new ideas and, in difficult circumstances, a real desire to embrace change in what is likely to be a rare window of opportunity for our country, our clubs and for every community in Scotland. While the game is anxious and apprehensive about the future, there have been many achievements and successes in Scottish football which we should acknowledge, especially when viewed against the size of our population and the extraordinary national emotion and ambition that our game has to deal with. That said my report pulls no punches and presents a dispassionate and candid assessment of the state of Scottish football and puts forward a set of far reaching reforms which are designed to reorder/renew/reform structures, governance organisations and priorities within the game in order to deal with current problems more effectively and embrace the challenges of the future. Change will always be difficult. But it has to happen.

Despite some positive achievements throughout the game in the last decade and a league structure that continues to attract relatively good attendances there is still a huge gap between our national ambitions for football and the success and achievements on the field. With our failure to qualify for any major international tournament since 1996, the European Championships and 1998, the World cup there is understandably a real sense of national failure and the fans and the public will rightly express their disappointment at the collective failure of the game to deliver.

What the review tries to do is to go beyond these obvious manifestations of underachievement and underperformance and ask some searching questions about the mind set of the game in Scotland and the structures, mission, ethos and organisation of Scottish football. The world of football is changing rapidly and if we are to build and maintain a competitive edge in club and international football then we have to learn lessons and be prepared to marginalise sectional or constituency interests within football for the benefit of the wider game. This is what the fans and the people of Scotland want to see. The difficult context in which the game finds itself holds out little prospect of an early easing of the extraordinary financial and economic pressures.

Our small population and our attendance figures, boosted enormously and also distorted by Celtic and Rangers, allow us to punch above our weight in terms of European rankings and coefficients but that of itself does not help the game overcome some of the formidable challenges that lie ahead. The review concentrates on what the game can do for itself and in doing so help football to become more attractive, more successful and be more effective in tapping the potential ,which undoubtedly exists to grow our club and national game. The key to this is sustainable finance, building more capacity within the game to deal with change and for the football institutions to have a much more open and transparent approach to new ideas and innovation. Our institutions are amongst the oldest in world football. The burden of history influences what we do and there has been for far too long a reluctance to embrace modernisation and make the game fit for purpose in the 21st century. So there is much to be done to change the way our national game is organised.

Much has been written about football in terms of day-to-day issues, controversies and the drama of fragmentation, indiscipline and self interest which too often distort the image of the game and precludes the promotion of positive things being done. The recent referees dispute is a classic example! All of this is understandable when some newspapers have 20 pages of football to fill every day but all of this impacts on the public perception of the game and leads to the conclusion – heard often in taking evidence – that the game is too preoccupied with itself and less concerned with the fans, supporters, sport and the wider frame of interests that the game relies upon for its existence. Humility isn't easy but the lack of it creates problems. This is why institutional inertia and the burden of history are real problems.

There is a need for the game to reconnect with its base and the people of Scotland in a more open, innovative and modern way. It is their game – the 3.1 million people who watched the SPL in season 2009/10, the three quarters of a million people who watched the SFL, the hundreds of people who watched our international sides in the past year and of course the vast army of armchair viewers. These people are the real shareholders of Scottish football and it is worth reminding ourselves that in Scotland we have the most loyal, long-suffering, and passionate fans in the world.

Our nation demands our international sides qualify in a consistent and sustainable way for the World Cup and the European Championships and that our top clubs do well in the Champions League and the Europa Cup. Few countries with small populations are as ambitious as Scotland in aspiring to achieve both strong clubs and national sides. This is a measure of the ambitious environment in which Scottish football operates but it is also the reason we need to change. If our level of national ambition is to continue, which is a very positive mind set for a country like Scotland, the game needs to change dramatically to close the gap between where we are and where we need to be!

My report makes no apology for being hard hitting about the state of our national game. As a 'passionate independent', I have been greatly encouraged by talking to a whole range of people who believe that change is needed. They often expressed the view that we need more self belief and that Scottish football is and can be much better that we would glean from the back pages of our newspapers. The Governance of the game has to change. The representative and participative structure of the SFA, the traditions, procedures and decision-making and the inherently defensive and insular approach of the organisation all present a serious obstacle to the modernisation of football in Scotland.

The present set up may have been appropriate and effective in another era. But today the pace of change, the financial pressures on football, the social and economic developments in society, the volume of day to day requirements and responses, the need for long term thinking and the need for informed policy and sound decision making represent a new world which requires a new modus operandi in the way we operate and in the way we deliver. Modernising the governance of the game is the central challenge of this review.

What does being fit for purpose mean in 2010? How do we create institutions and organisations that are effective and responsive? What is the purpose of football in the modern era? What is the game seeking to achieve for country, club and community? How can we retain the positive aspects of history, tradition, representation and sentiment in contemporary football? To answer these questions the review sets out in stark terms the concerns and criticisms that have been levelled at the current structures and organisation. These are based on the comments of clubs, organisations and individuals as well as representing a summary of my own views based on a thorough analysis of the institutions and in particular the SFA.

Football in Scotland has no overall vision and lacks a comprehensive and coherent set of values and principles and outcomes and objectives. Leadership and Governance and the structure, organisation and decision-making are crucial for the success of any organisation. Institutions have a vague, cursory and limited set of things they aim to do. There is a lack of effective formal consultation between the major stakeholders in the game and a lack of respect, confidence and trust. There is a distinct lack of confidence. The game is very fragmented and at times lacks any overall sense of direction. There is a great deal of insularity and exclusiveness. Decision-making is slow and delivery does not match the urgency and complexity of the issues involved. There is a great deal of personal, sectional and vested interest at work at the expense of the health and well being of the overall game. There is too much points scoring and as such the game generates a great deal of indiscipline and a lack of respect for the rules and regulations of the game.

A kind of tribalism operates and the highly informal consultation and dialogue that takes place between the institutions and their representative structures is no substitute for effective liaison, formal dialogue and cooperation. Decision making structures often lack focus and direction and compared with the best of the business sector are relatively ineffective. At times the game seems preoccupied with its own internal workings rather than the problems and challenges facing the game. Openness, transparency and accountability are lacking. The distribution of roles and responsibilities are confused and unproductive with the elected officials too involved in what s essentially the work of the Chief Executive and his management team. There is no real acceptance that the board takes strategic decisions and the Chief Executive is in charge of the day-to-day activities.

The game is too defensive and pessimistic and there is a great deal of grudge and grievance football politics. The committee structure may function for the benefit of the existing representatives but is ill-equipped and out-dated and is not able to deal with the modern world of football and the speed with which events and issues emerge and have to be dealt with. The game is also bigger than its component parts and personalities. Rules regulations and conventions should apply in equal measure to Chairmen, board members, managers, players, referees and personnel involved in the game... recent events have shown a remarkable degree of ill-temper, ill-discipline and vitriol rarely seen in a national sport. This should be a wake -up call. The game too readily seeks to blame others for its difficulties and on the back of more self- belief the game has to take more responsibility for its own shortcomings and its future.

There is no sense of modernisation and while there is some excellent work taking place within the SFA it is hard to see the current organisational structure allowing this to flourish. There seems little concept of public value and return on investment, permeating the SFA and once again the failure to reform decision making, policy and planning procedures and structure means that the full potential of the organisation is not being realised and incentives to change are simply not there. There is no performance culture within the SFA and for all intents and purposes the work is isolated in silos. It is constantly worth repeating that much of the weakness of the SFA is based on legacy and history and a traditional mind- set that surrounds the work of the institution. The shape and mould of the structure has largely remained intact despite the changes in personnel and the passing of time. But many if not all of the problems and difficulties within the SFA essentially relate to the overall structure, organisation and decision making i.e. Governance- in particular, how the key components interact and relate to each other.

Nearly a Decade On

Nearly ten years on from my review, the analysis of the game looks very similar. Significant changes have taken place, progress has been made on many policy fronts, committees have been streamlined and youth policy has evolved. But problems of culture, institutional inertia, long-term thinking, the lack of a unity of football purpose, a lack of strategic thinking and the lack of a bigger ambition and vision for the game, remain, but are currently off the agenda. Instead, the dominance of the Scottish Premiership, the archaic membership organisational structure, the isolated, exclusive and insular thinking, the unfair and unequal distribution of finance, power and authority within the game, the declining influence of the SFA and the lack of overall leadership and direction have all led to a crisis situation where the idea of an integrated, balanced and coordinated game seems to be receding.

Youth Talent: The Key to Success

The second part of my review was focused on talent development in the context of an expanding grass roots programme for girls and boys, and men and women. My case for the future of Scottish football largely rests on the concept of 'football capital' in the form of young people, representing as they do, the 'wealth of the game'. For far too long, Scotland has talked a great deal about the importance of young people and how our future depended on them but, in reality, the investment and inspiration required to achieve success has been lacking. Two powerful ideas must dominate our thinking, the common football good and the wealth of the game.

My review attempted to provide a practical and pragmatic set of proposals which would start to tackle some of the outstanding issues and address four important 'gaps': aspiration, ambition, achievement and performance, which then leads to a fifth, the talent gap. This area of talent development is where successful football nations have created a comparative, competitive performance edge. We thought that the 'Golden Age', where there was an endless pool of natural and indigenous talent, would last forever. It didn't.

What had been created is the result of the remarkable coming together of complex factors, which no longer exist. For me the review was a chance to use our unquestionable DNA, our love of the game and a very intense football network to help bridge all the gaps facing our game and create the best youth strategy in Europe. The game was calling out for ambition and I was confident there was momentum behind the idea as well as skilled and professional people to deliver it. I also believed that this was a unifying concept in a game that was lacking a unity of purpose. Nearly a decade on, I am apprehensive about what has happened to the dream. First, let's look at the ideas and recommendations in my report. Two areas stand out:, youth development and the link between football and the wider health, fitness and well being agenda.

Extract from 'Review of Scottish Football'

2010, details

Talent, Talent, Talent

This review urges a radical rethink of how we identify, manage, value and develop talent with emphasis on the "gold dust" quality of elite young athletes and the intensity of attention and provision we must give them if their potential is to be realised for the benefit of Scottish football, both the national and professional game. This is the distinguishing feature of comparisons between Scotland and our more successful competitor countries. Despite our deep-seated cultural ambivalence in Scotland to success, elites and the talented, we must now break out of this and accept our success now depends on a new mind set and the unashamed pursuit of excellence; building the base, identifying the talent and developing the potential.

Building a Consensus

There are however self-evident truths about a direction of travel that we can all agree on:

- The game is underperforming, underachieving and is underinvested and all of this contributes to our lack of success.
- We need a well thought out vision for the game, which brings together its disparate elements.
- Football needs to be a bigger part of the sporting revolution Scotland so badly needs.
- The transformation of the lives of children and young people and our contribution to fitness, health, wellbeing and confidence building are invaluable. This needs to be appreciated by a wider audience,
- Because of football's extensive networks, the potential role in the community is second to none,
- Government must become a much stronger partner in terms of building the base and the basics,

- The lack of grassroots facilities and football infrastructure are at crisis point,
- The grassroots game and youth development are under funded,
- The development of talent is the way forward,
- There is a lack of shared and quantifiable objectives and outcomes,

The Recommendations

1. The Scottish FA needs to provide more coherence, focus, coordination, direction, leadership and clarity to youth development.

2. An overhaul of the structure and organisation of the grassroots, recreation and youth game.

3. The winter break/summer football.

4. Football Academies - up to 30 based on comprehensive schools (there is a need for a new national academy of football/performance centre of excellence with the first priority being a new network of academies linked to education).

5. The appointment of a National Performance Director.

6. The appointment of an expert group on the development of the '10,000 hours' elite athlete concept.

7. A small review group to look at the 'duty of care and legal context' of issues relating to the rights and responsibilities of children and young people in the game including the issue of compensation A clearer and more extensive role for the Scottish FA in relation to the national game, including youth development with specific reference to regulation, oversight and the safeguarding of the interests of children and young people.

8. We need a new concept of the 'Golden Pathway' bringing together new ideas and innovation to develop elite athletes and youth talent. We need to add value to the existing pathways and make the process more transparent and focussed. There must be a far better partnership between the Professional Clubs and the National game.

9. The status of youth and talent development within the game must be raised and every professional club must have a youth framework and talent development programme.

10. To expand the base of the game and increase the numbers of children, young people and adults of both sexes playing football from the current figure of 366,000 to 500,000 (1 in 10 of the population) in five years.

11. A new commission to advance the 'Women's Game' in Scotland based on a more ambitious and sustained approach.

12. The new Scottish FA regions should be strengthened and become a more important part of the national game and work more closely with local councils.

13. Build a capability and capacity within the SFA to deal with Strategic Relations and the wider world of Sport and government.

14. We need the game to work more effectively in more joint efforts to identify, nurture and grow talent and ensure a more successful pathway to the top of both our national and club game.

15. Football must recognise the importance of sport, health, fitness and well-being in Scotland and seek to play a bigger part in promoting this revolution.

16. Our professional clubs and the Highland League, SOS and EOS should play a larger role in our communities. We need to develop the 'Sporting Club' concept and the idea of 'Football Enterprise'.

17. There are 14 recommendations for the government in relation to the sporting revolution we need and which will play a vital part in building grassroots football as well as providing healthier, fitter and confident children and young people. Sport overall will benefit from this. The importance of the government embracing these recommendations cannot be overstated. A great deal of work has been done but it must go much further. Without this sport and football will continue to have an uphill struggle in their search for talented sports men and women.

18. Scotland needs at least £400 million facilities and infrastructure programme for sport, including football over the next ten years. There has to be a new and urgent focus on the facilities gap, which has now reached crisis levels.

19. We need a new and different relationship with the Scottish Government especially in relation to joint programmes, youth development and further investment. A new partnership on health and sport is also needed. We need to reach out to the world of sport, re-establish the importance of schools in this sporting and football renaissance, recognise the importance of integrated education and football and to become key players in the fitness, health and well-being revolution.

Talent Recognition and Development

- The overall aim is to expand the base of grassroots, recreational and youth development. A great deal of excellent work is being done but we can do more. The wider the base the larger the talent pool in every part of Scotland and for both sexes.

- A new mind-set is needed towards talent development and practical reforms designed to tap the potential and close the achievement gap at the highest levels of the game. A greater degree of innovation and investment is needed.

- We should recognise the importance of government, local councils and schools in building the health, fitness and sporting revolution the country desperately needs in order to develop talented players and elite athletes.

- It is important to acknowledge that our professional clubs and national team are in a highly competitive game and that should encourage a more collaborative approach to the identification and nurturing of talent and the development of a more shared responsibility for the development of that potential. Part of that has to involve the education, personal and wider social development considerations of children and young people: as in most other areas of social policy this has to be built around a 'duty of care'.

- We do have choices. We can carry on as we are, and to use a phrase we can get by with minimum change taking tentative steps towards a better future. Or we can change our mind-set, modernise our approach, sharpen our thinking and improve both our competitive edge and comparative international position. This is the way to achieve a world-class status. This of itself can never guarantee success, but without it we will never escape the current sense of underachievement, underperformance, and lack of success. Part of this requires us to be constantly modernising our game and incorporating the best of European thinking.

- We should not underestimate the role of government. There is a great deal more that football can do to improve its current position: but without a more effective partnership with government this will be an uphill struggle. Government and local councils have resources

> both physical and financial and are involved in every community in Scotland. A new football-government partnership is vital.

Progress is Elusive

After having set out extensive extracts of the review carried out in 2010, much of the content seems as relevant now as it was nearly a decade ago. Covering both reports, over 100 recommendations were made and the vast majority of them have been implemented. But as recognised earlier, the game's problems were much more deep-seated. Some of the changes have made no appreciable impact on the fundamentals of institutional inertia, cultural constraints, lack of ambition and the seeming inability of the game to reach out of its comfort zone and link up with the world outside football in order to tackle some of the big outstanding issues. This raises the question of whether the game, in its current form, is capable of radical reform and whether it needs to face up to the uncomfortable facts that need to be confronted, before we can move on. How do we have a genuine debate in the country about what kind of football nation we want to be, and who should decide?

There are truths we must accept. The game, as currently organised, is not fit for purpose. The game no longer has any internal cohesion, direction of travel or sense of unity of intent or direction. The game is increasingly thirled to the needs of the few at the expense of the many, and this is getting worse. The SFA's authority is weaker than it was a decade ago. The Scottish Premiership is, by both intent and accident, narrowing the ambitions of the game, and has created an unfair and unequal distribution of income, power, authority and opportunity.

The archaic membership organisational structure is moribund as the limited power they once had, has drained away. The national team is given little priority and the short-term thinking surrounding this is holding us back. The game lacks any unifying themes. The game is not serving Scotland's needs. The game, if left to drift, will remain the focus of public criticism and sadly help drive its failure and decline from within. When the game started to decline seems far less important than identifying the date when it will start to revive.

There is one issue though that concerns me above all others, the youth strategy. This was the basic building block for the transformation of the game, but it seems to have run into difficulties. A new Centre of Football Excellence has been built. A performance structure and Director is in place.

There have been significant improvements at grassroots level. There has also been progress on the setting up of football academies. However, in recent months, there is every indication that progress has stalled and the original and inspirational thinking behind 'Project Brave' has been watered down, or even worse derailed, by a combination of the 'power grab', a narrowing down of ambition and a skewing of financial resources to certain clubs who can bid for the different levels of academies that have been created. There is also some evidence to suggest that the concept of regional academies is being side-lined, as the whole direction of thinking shifts back to the old clubs.

In the new structure, large parts of Scotland will not be served by an academy. Half of Scotland's 42 clubs will not play a part in the new structure and instead, we will have old and discredited ideas dressed up in the new language of youth development. There is talent in every part of Scotland and this should be recognised. Because clubs may not have the money to bid, doesn't mean they have no potential talent or are disinterested in finding it. The reality is different. The majority of Scottish clubs cannot afford to bid for academies, but those who can, prosper. It makes no sense to invest money and the ambitions of a nation into clubs where self- interest understandably comes first, and the needs of the national team come second. Finding talent is a Scotland wide issue and our greatest resource.

What is even more concerning is that the money we are about to spend on clubs who have considerable infrastructure and people, could be better spent on more worthy groups of clubs and other parts of Scotland. We shouldn't turn Project Brave into an exercise to continue the failed policies of the past. Many Scottish League clubs are struggling to survive and should be helped to participate in elite young player development. A national youth policy and strategy created by the SFA should be financed from the centre, and not from clubs who are struggling to survive.

Regional Academies and performance schools should be the centre of the youth strategy and Scotland-wide, not just where the existing centres of club power and finance are located. Every club in Scotland should have access to elite talent development. Each part of Scotland is capable of finding and nurturing talent; each child deserves the opportunity to achieve within their own area. Each family deserves the best, uninterrupted education for their child. Each community has the right of access to the best provision.

The future of our game does not uniquely depend on talented, young footballers only being developed in Glasgow or any other Scottish cities. Wastage rates among youth players are massive. Education is essential to keep the options open for all young people. Too many clubs are not willing to put the effort into developing young people and this has led to limited opportunities for Scotland's talented youth. There are no incentives for clubs to be interested; some may ask, why should clubs need them? The number of foreign players in Scotland means that fewer and fewer players are Scottish. As I said previously, foreign players will never play for Scotland. This is not the time for a new elite talent strategy to be stalling. This has become a serious club versus country conflict which gives rise to the much bigger and more fundamental question: in whose interests is Scottish football being run?

I am writing this chapter during the Germany versus South Korea and Sweden versus Mexico, hard on the heels of Denmark, Croatia and Uruguay qualifying for the last 16 of the Russia World Cup 2018. Our isolation and failure as a credible football country really hits home in these situations. Their talent, fitness, skills, strength, determination and natural ability shine through but I keep coming back to the simple question, why can't we do it? It is clear that relying on a few big clubs to nurture our young Scots, has failed. For at least the last 20 years, we have struggled on the international stage. To add insult to injury, the best opportunity in a generation to turn matters around, may be slipping away; fewer young Scots are playing at the highest level . This is a crisis. Our only road to future success is facing too many hurdles and time is not on our side. Our development of youth talent should include girls and young women. Gender equality is vital. It is again surprising that provision for them, originally included, has been taken out.

Who is shaping our future, clubs or country? Every part of Scotland should be asked to play their part in developing tomorrow's players. This should not be playing out as it is. A new start for the game was promised. While we need the clubs to invest in their own futures, the national interest needs a viable and effective system of regional based academies, performance schools, continuing education, and systems of oversight to ensure children are protected. The secretive workings of the game are not revealing any of this and we are left to speculate as to what is going on, and why the most important reform in a generation may have become another lost opportunity. We must move forward, but how do we unlock the undoubted potential that exists and, open up a new path to success? The final chapters will look at that question by offering a blue print for the future of the game. I will also pose the question of whether we want to make the tough choices that will be required. This requires exploring the identity crisis, deciding what to do about it and managing our approach to fixing it.

CHAPTER NINE

The Identity Crisis and What To Do About It

FOOTBALL IN SCOTLAND HAS ceased to be the product of its roots. One hundred and forty-five years since the founding of the SFA, the game has an identity crisis.

Different Times

Created in different times, in a world of vastly different lifestyles, football, like every other sport, must adapt and move on. The game in Scotland has many critics but, like myself, they love the game and want Scotland to succeed. I have attempted in this book, to show that we are a country of remarkable achievements reaching a high point in the '60s, '70s and '80s, in what can only be described as a 'Golden Age'. There is no doubt in my mind that Scotland has the potential to do well in the modern era and build, once again, a game worthy of its founding clubs, our obvious DNA and the passion and pride of Scots who may now be disappointed and feel let down but who would love to embrace success. Look at the impact of England reaching the semi-finals in the World Cup in Russia!

Scotland Needs to be There

For any one who doubts the importance of the 'beautiful game', I was enthused and inspired by the reaction of England to their victory over Columbia. Nearly half the population of their country watched on TV, it was party-time and a nation celebrated the success of a football match on the world stage. The pride and passion of a nation expressed through football. But I wanted it to be Scotland. We always think we have better fans than the English, so what if it had been Scotland clinching the penalty shoot-out? What might our reaction have been? Everyone would have been glued to their TV screens, the country would have come to a standstill and there would have been an incredible outpouring of national pride; the sense of achievement only success on the world stage can bring. This is the reality that fires my desire for the transformation of the game in Scotland. Scotland has the potential to be successful. It has nothing to do with the size of population. It has everything to do with the size of our ambition and the determination to put the national team – both male and female – as the number one priority and back that up with the best youth development structure in the world.

But the game and our country have a big choice to make. Carry on as we are and content ourselves with a modest league setup, and being dominated by one club or two or possibly five. Or look towards the creation of a new football regime where clubs can reach, and succeed, in European competitions and our men and women's teams can reach the final stages of the World Cup and The European Championships. Our history shows that this has happened before and so it is only our mind-set, limited ambition and the loss of identity that is causing so much unnecessary grief and disappointment. The club game can prosper in Scottish football, but not at the expense of the wider game or to the continuing disadvantage of our national sides and our desire to play internationally. The game must be rebalanced.

Small is No Excuse

Our confidence must be boosted by the success of smaller countries competing in the World Cup whilst having a small population. Of the 32 countries competing in Russia, more than a third of them had a population of less than 11 million. Of the countries in the last 16, slightly less than 50% of them had a population of less than 11 million. Of the countries in the quarter-finals, 50% of them had a population less than 11 million and two of them were much smaller than Scotland. There is a staggering reality that illuminates the reality of Scottish football. We are not good enough. Our game has become a pale shadow of its former self and a sad commentary on a country that deserves much better. Our national pride has been severely dented. Excuse after excuse has become a substitute for renewal and reform. The decisions that we have made as a game have put us here. No one else is to blame. Our downfall, our diminished ambition and our distorted priorities are the games responsibility.

Questions to be Asked

There are obvious questions to be asked and arising from the narrative so far:

What is the ambition for the game?

Whose game is it anyway?

Who decides its future?

What kind of game do we want?

How do we connect with fans and government and give them their say?

How do we effect change?

Opening Up

Part of the problem of Scottish football is its inability to reach out and connect with people that seriously want the game to be successful. The Scottish fans have an absolute right to a much bigger say in what is their game. In the modern era, governments have an important role to play, both in assisting football in a variety of ways, but also in football playing a major role in the sports, fitness, well-being and the health revolution that the country so badly needs. The internal structures, priorities and governance of football must change but opening up the game to the outside world is also important: the closed mind set and the suspicion of outsiders, are holding the game back and losing us valuable allies.

Incentive to Change

Is there the incentive to change in the corridors of football power? Changing an institution is far more difficult than making changes within an institution. My review in 2010 was about the latter, but today we must have a debate about institutional, cultural, and structural changes if we are to evolve the game and build a new future. The governance of the game is, in my estimation, not fit for purpose but the current game's narrow focus on the few and not the many, in particular the Scottish Premiership, could lead those whose narrow interests are being protected, to resist the deafening roar of those supporting change. This would be a pity as the club game is important and need not fear a more rounded approach to priorities and fairness within the game. Fear is a powerful constraint on change.

Is there willingness on the part of the clubs to recognise the unbalanced nature of the Scottish game and to be receptive to a much broader set of priorities, which better reflect the views of the fans and public? Is there a bigger agenda for the 42 league clubs, the majority of whom are concerned about financial survival rather than success on the pitch? Evidence would suggest that most of the clubs would like to see a more expansive approach to Scottish football but neither the structure of the game, their precarious financial position or the lack of effective democracy within the existing structure, allows this to happen.

New Thinking

Reinforcing the concern of clubs is the lack of effective forums within the game to express new ideas or new thinking. The structures of the game are a stark reminder of how little the game thinks out of the box, listens to fresh ideas or is able to innovate. The forums for dialogue and discussion are limited, reacting often to change but rarely suggesting change and only discussing issues that have been nurtured by the few and agreed using an archaic system of voting. Change will be difficult for the clubs. Institutional inertia is difficult to overcome.

Membership Organisation

Change will also be difficult because the SFA and the SPFL are membership organisations. If you were inventing the football authorities today, they wouldn't remotely resemble current structures. The mix of members and officials confuses matters. The overlap of responsibilities is complex. Elections are based on archaic procedures. Positions within the ruling bodies are arrived at in more military than modern procedures. There is no effective democracy and this in turn conveys the sense of a system being rigged and regimented rather than being responsive and relevant. This maybe harsh but even within the constraints of a membership organisation, things could be fairer and more demonstrably modern.

Defensiveness and Insularity

I do not overlook for a minute the respected procedures and traditions that dominate football and that have shaped the character of institutions for more than a century. But concessions must be made to modernity if the game is to tackle its obvious weaknesses, recreate in the modern era what the 'Golden Age' provided in another generation and have a forward and outward looking strategy of the future. There is no doubt in my mind that the extreme defensiveness and insularity of the game has become much worse over the last decade as failure has taken its toll of confidence and criticism has been shunned. This is neither sensible or helpful, but it does impact on the potential capacity for change within the Hampden headquarters.

These issues become important if change is to happen. The game had reached a low point in 2010, which created the opportunity for progress to be made. As the request for the review had come from within, there was a sense that recommendations would have a receptive audience. There is clearly a need for transformative change now but the prospects of new ideas being accepted are not encouraging.

Fans and Government

This raises the question of where the impetus for change comes from. I hope it will come from the game but it needs to be supported by the fans and the government. The government is in a difficult position but could become a positive force for change. It does not want to overplay its hand, as it is mindful of the 'no political interference' mantra of UEFA and FIFA. But, it is time to move on. There is a difference between political and governmental. Football should be free of party political meddling, but governments are a manifestation of public support, representing people and have a legitimate role to play, from the funding of youth football to dealing with sectarianism and bigotry.

Football needs to partner with government to help in tackling the health and sporting needs of Scotland; this is a new frontier for Scottish politics and the Scottish government. This would be the game reaching out to promote the wider interests of the nation. Let us not forget that a few seasons ago, the Scottish Government sponsored the League Cup and the common theme was health. These are real opportunities that have disappeared and need to be revisited. There is a role for the Scottish Parliament and its committee system. Cross party involvement is essential in providing an opportunity for debate and informed discussion.

The strained relations with the Scottish Government over a variety of issues have prevented further positive partnerships of scale. Scottish football is not an island unto itself and marking out a piece of Scotland and pretending that it doesn't need help or thinking that relationships with a democratically elected government and parliament are something to be avoided. It would be helpful if football was sponsored by positive ideas of health and fitness and not being overrun by the betting industry, which the English FA has agreed to phase out and which all governments are deeply concerned about. The Scottish game would argue that 'beggars can't be choosers' and suggest that is all that is on offer. What a dismal and depressing argument. If the game was modernised and presented in a more attractive offering, matters would be different with the game marching alongside the country and not in the opposite direction.

The Drivers of Change

Part of the thinking behind my case for change relates to the unfair and unequal distribution of power, finance, authority and opportunity within the game and the imbalance this creates in the direction of the organisation, and its priorities. If this state of affairs is the product of the ascendency of the clubs, in particular the Scottish Premiership, and the decline of the SFA, where does the impetus for change come from?

Although there are very few ways of assessing or measuring the public mood surrounding football, one thing is clear; this is more than a game or a sport or an issue of insignificance in the life of Scotland. Too big to fail, and too important to be left to itself to reform, it is surprising that there is no outside body or agency charged with any oversight or regulatory authority. Or is it?

Football has never been the subject of any effective official external public scrutiny, other than abiding by the law, being subject to the rules and regulations covering financial audit and adhering to business and commercial concerns. If the people of Scotland feel that football is letting them down, they have no recourse to anything other than to urge the game to listen and reform itself. The Scottish Government is reluctant to get involved and neither have they considered any form of external control being forced upon the game.

Westminster government ministers and the Sport, Media and Culture Committee of the House of Commons have threatened the English FA with action if reforms on certain issues were not considered. Nothing has happened but the degree of importance attached to the game, and its influence on important social and public order issues, has forced Westminster to adopt a much more aggressive approach towards what they believe to be a massive public body – the English FA – that seems to be beyond scrutiny and not accountable to anyone.

The idea of a Football Ombudsman has often been talked about as a first step towards more public accountability. Could this ever happen in Scotland? Clubs, with some exceptions, are businesses. They are responsible to their own boards and shareholders. They are also responsible to the SFA and the SPFL. But they are not often responsible to their fans – despite the fact they are the most important part of the game – or the Scottish public in any meaningful way. Ultimately, the fans and the public are represented by the parliament and the government, and it could be well the case that if long-term reforms are not undertaken on areas of common interest then the clamour for some form of public oversight will intensify. This should be an incentive for the game to reform itself and to accept how precious football is to a very wide cross section of life outside Hampden.

One example really helps illustrate the ongoing tensions between the government and the game. The behaviour at football matches, sectarianism and bigotry remain live issues. Remarkable improvements have been made by the clubs, the football authorities and helped by the government. But issues remain. The government believes the game could do more and the big clubs believe the government could do more. There is a huge public interest issue here. Sectarianism, bigotry, and racism are issues of universal concern and should be dealt with as such. Government and game should be at one on these issues. However, the clubs must accept that if they do more to combat these unacceptable attitudes in within their football grounds, then the government will get off their backs. Football is part of the mainstream of Scottish life and must act accordingly. Bigotry and sectarianism, on the other hand, must never be the occasion for party political division within the parliament. They remind us of the divisions that still exist today in Scottish life and which need to be stamped out. The game has made remarkable progress, but there is more to be done.

Isolated, Inward-looking and Exclusive

The 'circling of the wagons' is a well understood phrase. This is the default position of the football authorities when there is a whiff of trouble in the air. I am not quite sure why this should be within an organisation that is 145 years old. Organisations can be secretive, defensive and insular but not always. Lines of authority are blurred. Responsibility for decisions is never clear and the SPFL, SP and the SFA are increasingly overlapping organisations, far too informal in their relationships and too much sharing of the same members. This lack of formal boundaries and the informality of proceedings leads me to the suspicion that the SFA is losing authority in areas that are 'whole game' responsibilities and not those of the clubs, and in the process, declining in status as the clubs, especially the few, grow in authority. This is the most important reform to be undertaken; re-establishing the authority, importance, and credibility of the SFA. This is vital for pushing through further reforms, especially on youth development. Any new structure must have the SFA as the key to unlocking future success and the focus of the national and international game for both male and female. The club game is vitally important and should be viewed as part of the wider game. It doesn't work the other way around. The SFA must recover lost ground.

Resentment

Secrecy is something to avoid, especially if you are the subject of intense media and public scrutiny, every day of every week. Imagine the outcry if the Scottish Parliament always met in private, excluding media and public on every occasion and all comments, arguments and decisions were made behind closed doors. Could Scottish football not escape from its private world and open up many of its meetings and debates to the fans, supporters and the Scottish public? To have trust in an organisation, it must be open and democratic, and not in a grudging manner. The game is secretive and is very resentful of the interest shown in what it is doing. It remains incredibly precious of its right to remain silent until some manicured press release is given to the masses.

For example, I am very privileged to be the Chair of the Fife Elite Football Academy, which emerged from my report on youth development in 2010 and is now part of Project Brave. Officially, I have no idea what is happening to this project but unofficially I know that it has been derailed by the power of the few. The finance is being skewed to those clubs who may need it least and the idea of Regional Academies – the centrepiece of my thinking in the review of 2010 – is diminishing in importance. Scotland's DNA means we should be investing in every area of the country, but it would appear this is no longer the plan. Instead, if you have the finance as a club, you can win an academy while other areas of Scotland, covering nearly half of all the SPFL clubs, with little or no finance, will be excluded. The 'new thinking' seems to have returned to the failed, old idea of concentrating on the clubs. It is worth noting again that for 20 years, Scottish clubs have failed to provide the Scottish talent necessary to reach and participate in the final stages of the World Cup or the European Championships. If Project Brave has been derailed, then this must be a key reform in renewing the game. We must have a world-class youth development programme that will provide one of the missing pieces as we build a different, more European game in Scotland.

Reaching Out

There are ways we can reach out. Any reform of the game must reflect my idea that football is too important to be left to the game.

First, the game needs to open up, democratise, be accountable, reach out, inform and be inclusive. This requires new attitudes, confidence and a more trusting approach to the world beyond Hampden. There is a hostile environment; media criticism can be cruel and pervasive, and fans do wish to make their views known using every possible opportunity. But much of that happens because the game does not respond, has few channels of communication and is unable to distinguish between the constructive criticism and the negative vitriol. Frustration dictates a great deal of the angst and anger that surrounds the game but it should climb above this and reach out.

Second, the game must take a leap forward in embracing the importance of its fans and supporters, and in building a new partnership with government: they do not pose a threat to the game and are vital components of a football renaissance, long overdue. I have no idea why these relationships are so strained. Germany, despite their setbacks in the World Cup in Russia, is an enlightened country. Its post-war history, an informed and educated society and industrial ascendency mark it out as a modern nation with a great club and country game. Their fans are viewed as an integral and a vital part of the game, and are taken seriously. Why don't we have the same mind-set?

Third, Hampden HQ must realise that there is a larger world of football outside Glasgow. No-one denies that Glasgow is a formidable place with great clubs, great history, and the home of the national stadium, which has hosted some of the most epic football matches the world has ever seen. But much of Scotland feels left out and this is reinforced by much of the press and media coverage.

So, reforming the game must embrace, modernisation and democratisation: reaching out to fans and government, acknowledging that fans, clubs, players and the public in every part of Scotland have the same pride and passion for the game. Size is not everything!

What Success Looks Like

The case for transformative change seems overwhelming and the potential exists, but what would success look like and how would we define it?

My approach has been to deal with the politics, philosophy, and psychology of the game and to redefine its purpose in the 21st century. The mind-set of most organisations is complex and often defies easy analysis and simple solutions. In the case of Scottish football, the task may be easier to define, although the issues and influences throughout its long history are complex. The burden or the legacy of history is hard to cast off. Membership organisations make change and make reform very difficult: the fine balance of winners and losers may just lead to the status quo being preserved. The commercialisation of the game has had a massive impact and dramatically changed the distribution of power and income. The other side of the coin is the dramatic slump in the authority of the SFA, the failure of our international game over the last 20 years, our neglect of elite talent and our inexplicable inability to shape a world class youth setup.

Looking forward, these issues should dominate our thinking and help shape the institutions, culture, and structures of the game. In the eyes of a football loving country, the game has let them down and people feel frustrated and annoyed in equal measure. They feel the stature of the game has diminished. People need something to get excited about. We now have a lesser game than we had a generation ago. This is the only conclusion you can arrive at. But it doesn't have to be like this.

Our diminishing stature as a well-respected footballing country was made in Scotland. **Yes**, times have changed since the '80s, but we collectively failed to take the big decisions that would adjust our game and our thinking to the new challenges. **Yes**, more money arrived but we decided what to spend it on, and the national game, the most important aspect of Scottish football and the basis of national pride, has suffered. **Yes**, the conveyor belt of talent stopped, but why? After nearly a decade since I suggested a new youth strategy, have we made little progress, and fallen back on the failed idea that big clubs have all the answers to the crisis of youth talent? Have we then allowed the Scottish Premiership to be dominated by foreign players with few incentives for clubs to play young players? **Yes,** international football is always held up as being vital to Scotland so why then has the authority and power of the SFA been so weakened and its control over the game reduced? Who decided this was good for Scottish football? Were these changes made in the pursuit of a better game but resulted in unforeseen consequences? Or were these developments that were deliberately put in place, designed to change the face of Scottish football forever and see the few prosper at the expense of the many, and see the ascendency of the club game at the expense of our national and international game?

There is no doubt that our game has suffered in two ways. First, by accident or intent our game has changed. It seems that in the last 20 years we have collectively failed to recognise the symptoms of decline and as a result the game has lost much of its appeal. Second, it is also important to stress that in the same period the game has failed to respond to the challenges of the modern era has been left behind as Scotland moves confidently forward where our new politics has become a more powerful outlet for patriotism and nationalism and has failed to connect with many of the big issues facing both football and society.

The Nordic Experience

Learning lessons from other countries has never been our strong point. In a football world of fluctuating fortunes, the Nordic experience stands out. Size of population is not a problem. Indeed, having a small population may be a real advantage. Sweden and Denmark have been very successful and on a regular basis, have qualified for the final stages of international tournaments. Iceland has only recently made an impact, reaching the final stages of the World Cup and the European Championships, in the last two years. These are remarkable achievements for countries with 10 million people and 5.6 million respectively. Iceland's performance is sensational when you consider their population is 350,000! All of these countries seem to satisfy the description of football being a game of the mind, where legs and feet are merely tools: a high level of science, modern ideas and huge ambition.

These are modern small countries with progressive politics, high standards of living and a very civilised way of conducting themselves. Scotland's game developed in completely different social, economic, political, and industrial context. Their football development, however, is worth looking at. Scotland, today, is a very different country to what it was 30 years ago. In sharp contrast to the Nordic countries, we often argue in Scotland that our modernity –not enough poverty, can't play on the streets, heavy industry has died, children don't play outside and too much internet revolution – is one of the important reasons for our decline as a footballing nation. It seems logical, and slightly paradoxical then to look at ultra-modern Sweden, Demark and Iceland to see how they have managed to succeed in surroundings that are apparently so different from our Scottish past.

How did comfortable countries produce highly successful international teams capable of winning success, well beyond their population size and lifestyle? In so many ways, the modern post-devolution Scotland seeks to admire the achievements of the Nordic way of life and hold them up as a valuable model for the new (political) Scotland. Acknowledging the fact that our football history is very different, what lessons can we learn? Their club structures, and the importance attached to them, are limited compared with ours and seem less important in terms of national priorities. They do not have clubs as important and as successful as the 'old firm'. So the influences of power and finance are less distorting of their national game. Their efforts are focussed, to a much greater extent, on the national side. The thrust of my argument is that Scotland is moving in the opposite direction.

Their coaching, skill levels and facilities – vital in cold climates –are the envy of most countries. Smaller countries with less extensive league structures attempt to compensate by concentrating on aspects of the game they can influence, and which will provide the biggest return on scarce investment.

Despite the fact these countries are subject to the same rules, regulations and procedures of FIFA and UEFA, their football authorities seem to manage regular success at international level. Is it because they haven't the presence of a big-league mentality or do they just give a much higher priority to the national game? Much of the commentary on the Nordic success highlights a more focused mind-set and a clear national ambition. After qualifying for the World Cup in 1858, Sweden reached the final where they were beaten by Brazil – the first occasion the world was able to see Pele for the first time. Sweden have also reached the semi-final of another World Cup. Denmark, after failing to qualify for the 1992 European Championships, did participate after Germany were excluded. They reached the final and eventually won the tournament. How could that have happened? A country with the same population as Scotland became the European Champions? Our capacity to learn lessons is limited and we do not seem to have the ability to analyse in-depth, what similar size countries are able to achieve. Why can't we place 11 players on a pitch that can equal the achievements of other countries? These are historic one-offs cynics will argue. The facts don't bear that out. In our dark years, from 1998 to the present day, Denmark and Sweden qualify regularly for tournaments. Watching England versus Sweden in World Cup, Russia 2018 is proof, not only of getting into the finals but progressing to the quarter-finals. Denmark reached the last 16!

What drives countries to such success? There are obviously many factors at work but we must conclude that their ambition is not only big, it is backed up by a whole game approach that is unwilling to see their national effort undermined by the domination of club football. Probing deep into the anatomy of Scottish football suggests that we have given up on international success and, while we go through the motions of being a football-mad country, we have seen a collapse in self-belief and the kind of confidence that Jim Baxter took to Wembley in 1967 when we beat the victorious World Cup winners, England, and provided a textbook lesson in entertaining football. What is even more worrying is the possibility that we think we are giving our national side the highest priority and unlimited finance. If this is the case, then we are delusional and this requires a different response. Isn't it more accurate to conclude that, as a game, we are just failing Scotland and lack the kind of ambition that has taken other smaller countries to perform so well on the international stage? Some have put forward the ultimate argument that we may have just been unlucky... but for 20 years and how many more!

Another revealing feature of Nordic success is the fact that schools continue to play a vital part in their footballing success. Maybe it is time for schools to play a bigger part in our own youth development and incorporate some up-to-date thinking on how this can be achieved. The 2500 schools in Scotland are unique. This is the only place that every child must attend and so we have the most captive young audience in the world arriving in the same place for a decade of their lives. It is also the place where the health and well-being revolution can be promoted. There are so many positive reasons as to why schools matter. This is not turning the clock back; it is acknowledging that part of our underperformance is linked to our exit from schools, which in my days was the conveyor belt of youth talent. We could do more in our schools to develop our youth strategy, but football must adapt and reach out to them.

Iceland's success in global football is a dramatic wake up call to Scotland, as well as representing an inspirational call to action to lift our international game out of the historic low point it now occupies. For the game in Scotland to respond, Iceland should be viewed as a jolt to our complacency, but we need the humility to learn and act. Every day, anyone associated with the game must explain to themselves why a country, the smallest ever to qualify for the final stages of the World Cup and the size of the Kingdom of Fife, is world-class and a winner! I use these comparisons time and time again because while it says a great deal about Iceland. What does it say about Scotland? I am shocked, embarrassed and angry about our current plight. The solution is in our hands.

What is the magic elixir that provides the Icelandic sparkle, and seems to be sprinkled around Denmark and Sweden as well? Iceland was ranked 133 in the world four years ago, but today the national team has risen 100 places: largely because money and thought was poured into grassroots football. Scotland has also been spending on grassroots football and youth development, but it is difficult to assess progress.

Most football commentators stress the importance of mind-set, ambition and focussing on the things that matter. This all happened in Iceland in the last 15 years. We have been working on our youth development since the publication of my review in 2010, but we have still not pinned down an effective structure or model and Project Brave is struggling. Iceland's relationship with football has become an obsession, including the key players of the FA, government, schools, fans and the public. The ambition of the game is being shared by the nation and this provides a powerful incentive to succeed and massively punch above your weight. The lesson is obvious; how big is our ambition in Scotland and who shares it? Once a country shares a football ambition, it will be realised; this is the Nordic way. Working together in small countries is a vital part of football success. Scottish football needs the power and support of the wider Scotland to achieve its objectives but the game must change its mind-set. This is not meddling. This is not interference. This is not a takeover. This is not politicisation. It represents a new partnership model for the game to enjoy success on the international stage. There are so many areas where the interests of the government and football overlap; long term thinking, investment in the women/men and girl/boy game; youth development and grassroots; elite talent for both sexes; health, sport fitness and well-being; community development for club and country; facilities and affordable access; player education; and schools. The Nordic model is miles ahead of Scotland.

Coaching is the key; spreading excellence to a wider range of children and young people who can benefit, where the offer is open to people from any walk of life and becomes part of the culture. **Facilities** at local, club, community and regional level which are developed in partnership and include both indoor and outdoor pitches. Scotland has made some progress but it is not enough, and it lacks overall direction, coordination, and more effective involvement of local and central government. **Schools** in Nordic countries are the point of partnership and the obvious starting point, for both the priorities of national government and football.

Barry Rooney, writing in the Guardian in his article, 'Football: fire and ice, the inside story of Iceland's remarkable rise', said:

> My theory on why they are achieving, is that nowhere in the world do so many kids get practise as much per week, for as long, with a qualified coach in such good conditions. Just total enjoyment, total exhilaration.

Much of the television money is invested in this programme and based on shared priorities; government, schools, clubs, and national game. Rooney continues, '

This is as much an attitude as anything else. The things you need, but not the things you don't need. The most obvious application of this clear Icelandic model in England would be to go back in time 15 years and cancel the construction of the new Wembley. Spend that £757 million instead on land and facilities, spreading the ability to participate, put a proper workable open all week public pitch in every town and village. Watch all those other solutions to the same problems dissolve in its wake. The politics of small ambition goes hand in hand with our shemozzle of divided interests, the rise of market ideology across every aspect of public life. You get the strangled greed ridden systems of football you deserve.

In line with the spirit of these comments, my review in 2010 suggested that we open up our schools seven days per week and 52 weeks a year for sport (including football), fitness and health; resources which currently lie empty and unused for large parts of the year and for which we get no return on scarce public investment. Imagine a reality of massive resources lying unused for nearly six months in the year: this is Scotland in 2018. This recommendation was aimed at government and local councils and yet little progress has been made. In terms of ideas, this was a modest proposal but in terms of potential practical outcomes, this could be revolutionary; a scenario where a modest additional investment allows for the whole of our sporting school estate could be utilised – Nordic style. In a similar vein, and in the same review, I also suggested that half a billion pounds should be spent on new facilities, over the coming decade. Although there has been some impressive spending on new projects, it still falls short of what the country needs. This is where the size of ambition matters.

Other countries have big objectives, the courage and vision to back this up and the foundation funding that success requires. Scotland is simply not in that space. Long-term planning has to replace short-term thinking. Qualifying for the World Cup in Qatar in 2022 may be too ambitious, but why not the US/Canada/Mexico in 2026? Or a possible joint bid from the UK –the old home championship countries – in 2030. This is a great opportunity for Scotland to lead. There is some suggestion that after a European bid, China might enter the frame for 2034 World Cup (China has made a national commitment to win the World Cup by 2050). There are tremendous opportunities ahead for the Scottish game where we can enjoy, as we have seen in Moscow 2018, the incredible out pouring of national pride, excitement, and enthusiasm. When you factor in the European Championships in alternate years, there is a festival of football ahead and that could be Scotland's to enjoy. We must escape this era of diminished expectations and low ambition.

Any blueprint for the future of Scottish football, must contest the assumptions on which it is currently based. There is a rigged market set of financial conditions operating in the game which favours the few at the expense of the many, and as a consequence, is failing the wider football aspirations of Scotland and downgrading the work and historic responsibilities of the SFA. They are undermining our international aspirations, failing to deliver a world class youth and elite development programme and, overall, failing to connect with an outside world that is keen to help, but is prevented form doing so. Any serious attempt at renewal must tackle the institutional inertia, the cultural constraints, the poor structures of governance and the lack of national ambition that are holding us back.

The Nordic countries do not have our remarkable football history; a 'Golden Age' of unequalled success on the international and European stage, attendances that still dominate world records, some of the greatest managers and players of the 20th century, two giant clubs, Rangers and Celtic, with competition from a 'new firm', Aberdeen and Dundee United in the 1980s. However, they are examples of modernity and they are able to harness their football capital, reach out, capture the national mood and brilliantly organise 'young talent'.

This discussion about the Nordic countries is important. Each country is different, with Iceland unique in world football. But setting aside their motivation and psychological makeup, their long-term importance to Scotland is obvious. We bemoan the fact that our 'Golden Age' has gone and we argue that it is impossible to recreate the social, economic, and industrial conditions that created it; leaving aside the political and religious issues that helped shape much of what we do. But Scotland is now a modern progressive social democratic country, similar to our Nordic colleagues, so why can't we do what they are doing? Why does Scotland find it so hard to learn anything? For reasons that we have teased out in this personal view, we shouldn't, by any stretch of the imagination, be in this dismal position.

Same Old Thinking, Same Old Results

The success of small countries exists outside the Nordic nations. Uruguay (3.3 million people) and Croatia (4.1 million people) have thrived in the World Cup in Moscow, reaching the quarter-finals and semi-finals, respectively.

They also have something to teach us. Instead of this barely credible, but much argued, mantra of excuses – no streets, no religion, no sectarianism, no poverty, no class consciousness, no children playing outside, and no schools – combined with the argument that the digital revolution is forcing children and young people to sit all day and play with iPads and iPhones to the exclusion of healthy outdoor pastimes, why can't we admit that the post-1998 era must end so we can build a new future?

We have, on the one hand, countries with small populations like Croatia, Serbia, Costa Rica and Uruguay with issues such poverty, material deprivation and hardship, who can qualify for World Cups. On the other, we have the Nordic countries with small populations like Sweden, Iceland, Denmark and Switzerland, who are progressive, wealthy, healthy and who qualify for International tournaments. Scotland can describe itself in any way it wishes, but the reality is that size, economic conditions or standard of living are no bar to footballing success on the international stage.

Case and Cause

There is no plausible case to explain our decline. Instead, narrow causes have conspired to alter the face of Scottish football at the expense of a more ambitious and expansive game. Every nation is different, and we cannot transfer a complete model from one country to another. But there are key parts of each of their approaches that we can incorporate.

How We Play

Any international tournament will reveal different styles of playing the game, different levels of physicality and various tactics and organisation. The play of teams like Spain, Argentina, Brazil represent a tight passing, close-knit game with considerable individual skills is one style for example, and of course, there are variations on every basic style. Increasingly, World Cups show the well-organised, tough, strong, hard and fit teams, who rely on the break, and with less reliance on 'ball skills' or individual brilliance. While these are arbitrary and rather crude descriptions, they do reflect Switzerland, Russia, Iceland, and Sweden in the most recent World Cup.

What is the Scottish style? It could be argued that there is a UK style as developed over a very long period and shaped by the enduring competition of the Home Championship, which dominated football, for many generations. In Scotland, excellent coaching is producing far more 'ball skill'-conscious young players who have more tactical awareness, mindfulness, passing ability and fitness. These qualities will be increasingly evident if clubs exercise more interest in playing young Scots as they come through the coaching process and have the incentives to do so.

At both club and international level, does Scottish football fall between the two simplified versions of the game that I have outlined? Gordon Strachan in a post-match interview after we had failed to qualify for the 2018 World cup, started to talk about this by referring to DNA, and in a broader interpretation of what he was saying, physicality. To some extent, he struck upon an important theme. From the perspective of an enthusiastic friend of the game, I am still surprised that so much of our football doesn't originate with the goal-keeper throwing the ball out to a colleague and, instead, sending it long up field with no intent behind the move. I am equally interested in the fact that too many throw-ins are sent down the touchline, instead of finding a player. Build-ups from defence are often few and far between. The mid-field is often bypassed. The long chasing ball is the chosen method of attack. Holding on to the ball seems difficult and there is a great state of hurriedness, which exudes an anxiety and lack of confidence.

My impressions of how the game is played may be offline and overly critical but I remain concerned about style in a world when so many countries are improving and the quality of playing increasingly reflects the new game, where football is essentially a mind game where feet and legs are the tools. This brings me back to points raised earlier about short-termism, the excessive turnover of managers and the lack of an integrated approach to our international game as well as bringing together all the levels and age groups for both males and females. I am not sure that Gordon Strachan was responsible for our failing to qualify but, as in previous years, he left, probably adding to a long list of unfinished work that simply slips from one manager to another.

An integrated approach would require national and international football to be the dominant priority in Scottish football. This must be followed by a transformation in the way we organise the national sides of both sexes, the youth development and elite academy programme, the Director of Performance, the managers or coaches of both the men's and women's national side, an 'ideas, learning and overseas think tank' facility and finally, a commitment to a sustained long-term strategy which has the support of government, the fans and a buy-in from a wider set of Scottish interests. We have to shift the mind-set and stop seeing this process of qualifying every two years for international tournaments as just another item in the football calendar that has to be done. Scots, and the Scottish teams at every level, have to be convinced that playing for your country is the apex of the game and that international success is a remarkable boost for country.

It is hard to escape the facts and thats why they are worth repeating: 10 reasons why Scottish football is in decline.

- Scotland is not keeping up with spirit, mood and innovations of other small countries.

- We don't need to create the conditions of the past to produce the football stars of the future.

- We do need to create the environment in which young Scots, of both sexes, can shine and start to dominate the football of tomorrow in a modern context.

- There is a depressing, and some-what self-serving and convenient tone to much of the excuses being used to explain away our national decline.

- Why is it not possible to have a 'Golden Age' in the 21st century when other small countries are doing this?

- The Scottish Premiership dominates our game; the barely concealed collapse of the membership organisation and money, supposedly running the game.

- Compared to the Scottish Premiership, the national/international game increasingly looks like a lesser priority.

- Our hopes for a new world-class youth development programmes have been derailed and sucked into the resource feud between clubs, at the expense of a new system of regional academies, for both sexes and for all clubs.

- The slow but increasingly rapid run down of the SFA and its authority.

- Over time we have moved out of the orbit of the wider Scotland and have become very remote from national aspirations and modernity.

CHAPTER TEN

What Next and How to Fix It

THE GOVERNANCE OF THE game may have been appropriate and effective in another era, but it is inappropriate for modern times. The representative and participative structures, the institutions, the culture, the traditions, the procedures, the systems of accountability and decision-making, the inherently defensive, exclusive, and insular approach of the organisation all present serious obstacles to the modernisation of football in Scotland. The modernisation of the governance of the game is the central challenge facing us today and it is also the key to unlocking Scotland's football potential.

Scottish football lacks vision, direction and ambition and is often devoid of a national strategy and plan. This allows vested interests to pull the game in different directions, taking advantage of a weak membership structure which benefits the few, and which is removed from any serious decision-making, policy development or influence. It also allows key and potential allies to be excluded such as the government and the fans. The distribution of finance, power, authority and opportunity, needs to be revised. The reprioritisation of the national game is long overdue and we must establish a world-class youth development and elite strategy. Making this work requires the SFA to reassert its power and authority to shape the future of the game, unencumbered by the widening net of SPFL thinking and the steadily growing influence of the Scottish Premiership.

To make these changes we must create a unified structure for the game, establish one key overarching body which gives direction and national planning, which at the same time brings together the disparate strands of the game to make a bigger contribution than merely the sum of the various parts. The game needs to reach out, be transparent, less secretive and more inclusive. These changes would send a powerful message about the serious intent and willingness of the game to face a future where success, not failure, dominates our football. Internal coherence would make a significant difference and would allow the outside world to make more sense of how football works. Scottish football is going nowhere unless it rebalances its priorities and radically reforms its organisation.

Big questions dominate the debate. How do we create institutions, organisations and structures that are hungry for success and able to make our game effective and responsive? What is the purpose of football in the modern era? What is the game seeking to achieve for country, club, and community? How can we retain and use the positive qualities of our history in contemporary football?

Personal Journey

My personal football journey has looked at the anatomy of the game, discussed the politics, philosophy, and psychology of what is happening and argued that football could have a successful future. But this can only happen if we pursue radical and transformative change that puts the interests of the whole game above any narrow or special interests. Success must be based on a game that reaches out and builds partnerships with the fans, government – both central and local – and the wider Scotland. An expansive, ambitious and inclusive way forward is essential. Change is difficult, uncomfortable and can be threatening, but it must happen.

I have been candid in my assessment of both the problems and the potential, and passionate about where Scottish football is today and where it needs to be tomorrow. Today, the pace of change, the competitive atmosphere, the financial pressures on football, the social and economic developments in society, the challenges of the digital revolution, the volume of day-to-day requirements and responses, the need for long term thinking, sound policy and sound decision making; all of these factors represent a totally different world that requires a new modus operandi in the way we operate. There is a need for the game to reconnect with the people of Scotland in an open, innovative, and inclusive way. People are the real shareholders of Scottish football and it is worth reminding ourselves that in Scotland we have the most loyal, long-suffering, devoted and passionate fans.

Few countries with small populations are as ambitious as Scotland in aspiring to achieve both strong clubs and national sides. This is a positive approach but it also reinforces the need for change and to appreciate the scale of the challenge. The national game is losing out and we need to rebalance Scottish football, raise the importance of the national side then close both the aspiration and expectations gaps between where we are where and we need to be. Our institutions are amongst the oldest in the world and inertia, along with the burden of history, weighs heavily on what we do. But one thing is clear: if we are to build and maintain a competitive edge in club and international football then we must learn lessons and be prepared to control sectional or constituency interests within the game for the benefit of the 'common good'. This is what the fans and the people of Scotland want to see.

Understanding Our Weaknesses

To make progress we must escape the blame culture that so easily becomes a substitute for reasoned analysis and which, in turn, so easily accommodates short-termism and failure.

- We can't blame population size.

- We can't blame the government, as they remain a largely unused resource.

- We can't blame our harsh climate, although playing in the winter weather is not the best way to develop skills and make the best of our talent.

- We can't blame the fact that too few Scots play in the Scottish Premiership, when we provide so few opportunities for young Scots to perform.

- We can't blame the government for lack of investment when they are suspicious about what we do and are confused as to why we are not spending more football money on the real priorities of the game.

- We can't blame the lack of pride, passion and ambition; Scotland has this in abundance.

- We can't blame the clubs for trying to achieve success in a competitive and difficult financial environment.

- We can't blame our fan base as this remains a brilliant, but a mainly unused asset, who have been loyal to the clubs and country in difficult and turbulent times.

- We can't blame the lack of finance as this reflects market size and the quality of the product on the pitch. More to the point, how is the finance being used?

- We can't blame the media for their often negative, pessimistic and sceptical coverage of the game, bearing in mind they produce acres of news print and reflect, to a large extent, the frustration of the fans and an often downbeat mind-set, which is strangely reminiscent of other aspects of Scottish life.

Measured against our 'Golden Age' of football nearly a generation ago, our game is under-achieving. Other countries have adapted, new countries have emerged and overall, footballing nations around the world seem in good shape relative to Scotland. What has happened in Scotland reflects choices that have been made by the football authorities over the last 30 years. The state of the game today is not an act of God or an act of nature, or the unintended consequence of the actions of one person or another. It is the result of serious neglect, a casual dismissal of what the rest of the world was doing and a narrow embrace of club over country.

There is an alternative scenario that suggests we look inward and take responsibility for the state of the game and collectively plan a new future. But this raises a fundamental point. Can we change our mindset and envisage a football renaissance in which we trade a comfortable, contented and complacent attitude towards the wider game for a more ambitious whole-game approach that will win success on the international stage and recreate, in the modern era, the success and achievements of our 'Golden Age' nearly a generation ago? Fanciful and deluded could be used by some to describe this state of mind. I disagree. Having watched Croatia – population of 4.1 million – beat England in the semi-final of the World Cup 2018, I see another future for Scotland. But it needs a revolution of ideas and thinking, a national football plan, plenty ambition, long-term staying power and a massive determination to succeed.

Sports excellence must triumph over sports power and finance. Of course, football is a business. But our business approach over the last 20 years has not delivered success on the international stage for club or country and it has not produced a pipeline of talented young players. Instead, it has manged to undermine the authority and provenance of the SFA and created an unfair and unequal distribution of finance, power, authority and opportunity within Scottish football. This has created a lesser game. If these developments are not contested then the enthusiastic domestic scenes in other countries that have accompanied World Cup success in Russia will never be experienced in Scotland. This is where we are heading.

What are the Challenges?

An excellent submission from HF Moorhouse of Glasgow University, to a Scottish Parliamentary inquiry into Scottish football in 2005 sums up many of the issues raised in this book. Talking about the effectiveness of the current structure, which has changed little since then, Moorhouse said:

> Effectiveness cannot be judged without some broad agreement on exactly what we want the organisation to achieve. This is helped by achieving some consensus on the aims and objectives of Scottish football. In short there is no current, comprehensive, coherent vision or national plan for Scottish football as a whole. This must be remedied as a vital part of creating a unified structure for the game and a base for building consensus, confidence and trust around our direction of travel. Other countries in Europe have reviewed their structures and practices and altered them on the basis of a plan for future development with agreed aims. Form would then follow function. No such provision exists in Scotland and so policy seems to be reactive, driven by short-term crisis and perceived opportunities, rather than forming a proactive, long term strategy. **If the game lacks an agreed set of aims then this allows each constituent part to pursue its' own aims and agenda which can create tensions and conflict and lead to an inefficient use of resources, lack of transparency and clarity and fragmentation of thinking and policy delivery. There are various bureaucracies within the existing structures of the game with their own objectives and agendas. There are vested, sectional and constituency interests which have become a major barrier to structural and organisational change.** What it need is central direction and leadership of the game. There is a need for a vision, a plan for realising the vision and then a dynamic intent to implement the plan.

The comments in bold highlight the need for central direction, a national football plan along with leadership, both in and outside the game. The future will be shaped by governance – institutions, structures, culture and organisation – along with the themes of unity of purpose and mind-set.

What would this look like? I have outlined **20 ideas** we could use to develop a healthy and successful game which:

- Establishes the primacy of the SFA, its provenance, authority, and power;

- Addresses the issues of narrow, special and vested interests which are distorting priorities, favouring the few at the expense of the many and destroying the idea of an integrated approach to effective governance;

- Gives meaning and substance to the idea of a 'membership organisation' where democracy, participation and having a real say would become a reality and openness, transparency and accountability would be the natural order of operation;

- Halts the constantly expanding power of the club game, especially the Scottish Premiership, whilst protecting their autonomy and ability to build club success but not at the expense of the wider game. The idea of a more holistic and unified approach to the game will only take root if the game is rebalanced;

- Builds bridges to the outside world and casts off the cloak of secrecy that too often alienates those who wish to help;

- Removes short-term thinking and builds our international game – for both sexes – as the number one priority facing Scottish football; let us nurture the self-evident truth that, in football terms, Scotland is bigger than any one club or all of the clubs;

- Regularly qualifies for the final stages of the World Cup and the European Championships, for both sexes. This has been brought into sharp focus recently by the World Cup in Russia and our continuing failure to qualify for any international tournament in the last 20 years;

- Starts to acknowledge the importance of fans and their need to be drawn more closely into the fabric of the game;

- Delivers a competitive and thriving professional club game where finance is secure and stable, and punching well above the size of our population in European tournaments;

- Establishes a world-class youth and elite talent development programme as the most important priority facing football and commits to building a programme based on the best facilities – the equal of any in Europe – and coaching, alongside the broadening and deepening of our grassroots and recreational game;

- Promotes Scotland as a beacon of best practice and the elite of Scottish footballers being regarded as top-class players around the world, sought out by the best clubs in Europe;

- Acknowledges the importance of the game to every community, in every part of Scotland and takes steps to maximise the potential for sport and civic renewal;

- Is aware of the wider contribution football makes to the improvement of the health, fitness, confidence building and well-being of the nation, and aspires to be a key part of the health revolution Scotland so desperately needs;

- Reaches out and builds new partnerships with government – central, local and wider Scotland;

- Values the role football plays in building character, responsibility, and respect across the age groups;

- Understands the importance of football for national pride and the Scotland brand;

- Acknowledges the problems of inequality and poverty in Scotland and seeks to work with government as a partner in tackling the problem;

- Continues to address the problems of bigotry, racism and antisocial behaviour;

- Recognises the importance of the women's game and the increasing contribution this will make to the growth in overall grassroots participation and international success.

If pressed, the game will always argue that these ideas are being pursued, in one way or another. Similarly, when at the sharp end of any criticism about the state of the game, the football authorities are very keen to remind myself, and others, that virtually all my recommendations from my 2010 review have been implemented. But to what extent, with what degree of resource, with what priority, with what urgency, to whose benefit, with whom, and with what degree of commitment have they been delivered? The overarching question that captures the thrust of my concerns is, in whose interests is Scottish football being run? Making changes within an organisation is much easier than changing the organisation itself, especially when it is the problem. This is now the outstanding challenge.

The organisation, the institutions and the culture are not fit for purpose. We are dealing with a mind-set shaped by history; foundations that were built in the 19th century, modest developments during the 20th century and caught up in a downward spiral in the 21st century that has continued to the present day. Viewed from inside the corridors of power, a different perspective will be on offer, which may rail against the idea of radical change and argue instead that the modern Scottish game is beset by a tsunami of changes that make the kind of reforms and rebalancing that I am suggesting, out of the question.

Accepting this will mean:

Giving in to the **politics** of defeat, sacrificing the possibility of a very different future and bowing to the well known Scottish trait of being a victim of the actions of others, or accepting the notion that all of this is inevitable as the pace of change in our troubled world accelerates or as society changes people have more to do with their valuable time than watch football.

Accepting the **philosophy** of a lesser game with diminished expectations, a culture of contentment, a poverty of ambition and an endless stream of excuses as the game declines further and a narrow game for the few sees international success as a distant memory and the product of our 'Golden Era' is never to be repeated.

Embracing a football **psychology**, which has already taken root, and which would flourish as part of a limited mind-set and psyche, which would ensure the behaviour of the clubs would be highly protectionist to the exclusion of the wider game and the true interests of the fans and country.

Football's dismal future may not be too wide of the mark but it does not chime with the positive embrace of a footballing future I hold dear. After a long association with the game, a respect for the ideas that fired our founding fathers, our pre and post war success and the undoubted potential that still exists in our DNA, I am convinced that a significant future lies ahead but only if we take radical steps.

Setting out the Debate

Themes Underpinning a New Future and The Scale of the Challenge

How fitting it is, with World Cup still in our minds, for me to use a poem, 'No Man is an Island' from a 17th century English poet, John Donne, to capture the plight of Scottish football in the 21st century. The first few lines read,

> No man is an island,
>
> Entire of itself,
>
> Every man is a piece of the continent,
>
> A part of the main...

Scottish football must break free from its self-imposed isolation. There is an important subtext to this theme. The Scottish Premiership has become an island entirely of itself and it too must connect, not only to advance its own interests, but to help rebuild confidence and trust in the game.

The second defining theme is that the game is too big to fail. Despite maybe falling short of the Bill Shankly 'more important than life itself' analogy, the game's importance to Scotland must never be underestimated. The Russia World Cup is testament to the impact of international football, not only on the fans, but the general public. The English teams' World cup performance has brought people together, provided an outlet for pride and passion and, however temporary, has united the country. Scottish football is more important than we think.

The next theme is the idea that the future of the game is too important for it to be left to the football authorities to control entirely. The game will struggle unless it allows the outside world to come in and help: ideas, inspiration and experience exist in abundance, but it is rarely sourced. Critical friends are priceless assets in times of difficulty, so they need to be used. Scottish football needs help.

Theme four is fear. Franklin Delano Roosevelt, President of the United States, once said,

> The only thing we have to fear is fear itself – nameless, unreasoning, unjustified terror that paralyses needed efforts to convert retreat into advance.

Scottish football seems insecure and has retreated into an increasingly small zone of comfort where the intrigue of football politics may be a boon to a small number of journalists on the inside, but where the masses on the outside remain out of touch with the game and don't feel part of what is happening. Scottish football needs to stop being fearful and start to engage.

Finally, we must acknowledge the common good of the game. Unifying concepts and themes are thin on the ground. Our game is a collection of disparate elements, fragmented and lacking any overall cohesion. The growth of competing interests has destroyed any unity of purpose and the notion of shared aspirations. Scottish football should preach the idea off the common good.

Principles To Be Followed

Reforming membership organisations is complex and arduous. Institutions, cultures and structures are complicated and so are the many informal relationships and conventions that make them work. Scottish football, to make an effective contribution to 20th century Scotland, must alter the way it operates. To do this we need some principles that will resonate with those who are charged with the transformation of the game. Principles will help to strengthen the identity of an organisation and its various institutions. These in turn will provide the basis for gaining respect and trust as well as being helpful in measuring progress; principles are timeless. The game must be:

Accountable

To both its members and associates but also subject to outside scrutiny and oversight. Fans, government and the wider public may want to have a role in this, bearing in mind the considerable interest and investment the game receives.

Democratic

In terms of how the various parts of the organisation function in order to ensure parity of esteem, equity in the distribution of resources and equality of access in relation to policy-making and decision-making. The 'for the few, not the many' approach doesn't fit. A deeper democracy means more than a vote at any AGM.

Inclusive

Far too many organisations and individuals, including fans and government, remain shut out from the game and feel football is disconnected and remote from the sweep of important issues, which matter to both the game and society. Bridging gaps and building partnerships will help Scottish football.

Transparent

It is difficult to understand the way football operates with most of the decisions being taken behind closed doors. This excessive secrecy creates mistrust and opens the game up to criticism, which may not be justified but is generated by the behaviour of the institutions and the frustration of those who want to help. The committees of the Scottish Parliament meet in public and have sessions when the public can get directly involved. Cabinet decisions are open to the scrutiny of the MSPs, the media and ultimately to the people.

Connected

This has been a constant theme running through my arguments for change. Connectivity in the modern age is everything. The fans are the real shareholders in Scottish football but links with them could be described, with some notable exceptions, as extremely tenuous and not valued by the decision makers. At club level there have been positive developments, but the concept of connectedness is not the priority it should be throughout the wider game.

Fairness

This is a tough concept to pin down but the distribution of power, accountability, finance and opportunity within the game is not fair or equal, and neither are the archaic voting procedures that benefit the few, not the many. Respecting the fact that the Scottish Premiership is the money generating element of the club game and within which we have the power of the big five, there is still scope for fairness from the point of view of justice being done as well as being seen to be done. A system that seems to be permanently rigged against you, will generate criticism and discontent.

Unifying

There is nothing unifying about the game in its current form. Fragmentation is obvious. There are few connecting threads made worse as members, officials and overlapping committees with overlapping membership seek to make sense of issues rarely discussed outside Hampden. Lines of authority and responsibility are blurred, vested interests are protected and decision-making is never transparent or subject to any serious form of external scrutiny or validation.

Immediate Priorities

1. The Common Good

The idea of the 'common good' of football has relevance to how we view the game. An article by *Newsweek* columnist, Robert J Samuelson said,

> We face a choice between a society where people accept modest sacrifices for a common good or a more contentious society where groups selfishly protect their own benefits.

It is worth adapting this idea to football. The philosophy of the 'common good' originated over 2000 years ago in the writings of well-known football supporters such as Cicero, Machiavelli and Jean Jacques Rousseau. The common good means a rejection of football operating on the principles of for the few, not the many and the narrow pursuit of vested interests. We must challenge these ideas if the game is to survive and flourish. Adopting the idea of the common good is both philosophical and practical. We currently have many different games pulling in different directions with no sense of the common good of the game. There is no unity of purpose, only fragmentation and discord.

At a philosophical level, the game needs to rise above money and materialism and consider what we want to build and how we can attract children and young people to what is essentially a sport for them, and not just a business. Football often seems remote from the notion of the common good, caught between the market aspects of the game on the one hand and the bureaucracy of FIFA and UEFA on the other. In all of this, football must be rooted in Abraham Lincoln's 'of the people, for the people and by the people' concept when talking about good governance. Football is moving further away from its origins and there is a tendency to believe that there is a sense of entitlement operating, that no matter what happens to the game, public support and the devotion of the fans will remain steady. There is no guarantee that this will happen. With humility, the game must adapt its thinking and see the idea of the common football good as a powerful unifying idea and an alternative to rampant commercialism and the worship of money: the saturation of the Scottish game with betting industry sponsorship is the most obvious example of how far we have removed ourselves from the common good of both the game and society.

2. Empower the SFA

Secondly, we must empower the SFA to establish its power, provenance and authority within the game. The SFA *is* the game and every aspect of football should see itself as part of this, complementing and not competing. The SFA must be the powerful voice behind the common good of football and to act as a unifying force at a time when the game is increasingly unfocussed, fragmented, and lacking direction. The authority of the SFA has been badly undermined. It must once again be the face of football, able to shape and influence the game with the help of the clubs, but not dictated by them, and make decisions that are dictated by long-term need, not short-term fixes. More bluntly, the SFA must halt the power grab of the Scottish Premiership, curtail the encroachment of the club game into decisions that are of wider significance to football and actively intervene to prevent the current iteration of our youth development strategy, Project Brave, being shaped by the failed ideas of the past.

3. The SPFL

The third priority is promoting the interests of the SPFL but at the same time drawing a sharp distinction between the legitimate ambitions of our clubs and their ongoing ability to eat away at the authority of the SFA, exert their own priorities and gain narrow advantages at the expense of the wider game. The national game is bigger than the club game. I accept that the clubs are businesses but we are at a point when the battle between sporting excellence and sporting power must be resolved: not everything that is done by the clubs is in the interests of Scottish football or the wider Scotland. The club game must become part of mainstream thinking on a range of social, cultural and justice issues – equality, gender, child protection, human rights, children and young people, dementia, gambling and betting, diversity, inequalities, living wage, bigotry, sectarianism and racism. Progress is being made, but there is still a tendency for the club game to plead exceptionalism and uniqueness and generate the impression that these wider aspects of life may not apply to them. This doesn't make sense. But it does help explain the frustration of government in their many dealings with the football authorities. The autonomy of the SPFL should be guaranteed but not through joint boards unduly influencing the game and by usurping the authority of others.

4. Elite Youth Development

Next is the issue of youth development strategy and elite talent development. After recommending the idea in my review in 2010, I am very concerned about what is happening. 'Project Brave' is the working title and has been a little tarnished by recent events. It has been derailed and we are in danger of turning the clock back and returning to the same old thinking which will inevitably produce the same old results. This issue is vital for the future of Scottish football, the performance of our national sides and the prospect of winning again on the international stage.

Originally the restructuring of youth development was based on a Scotland-wide approach, reaching out to all clubs and creating a network of Regional Academies. What now seems to be happening is a much smaller ambition – dictated once again by the important clubs, the few – with nearly half of Scotland's 42 clubs excluded, half of Scotland, the country, excluded, a concentration on clubs that can afford to bid for the available cash if they satisfy the UEFA criteria and the near abandonment of the Regional Academy concept. There is an absurd proposition behind this, namely the idea that the ability to finance a bid equates in some way with the availability of talent.

This thinking is fundamentally flawed. Does this mean that because a club doesn't have the finance, it is neither interested nor willing to participate, or more to the point has no talent in their area that they want to nurture and develop? There is nothing in the law of football economics to suggest we equate lack of money with a lack of talent. Those who have the most and shout the loudest at the headquarters in Glasgow are creaming of the cash and, in many instances, strengthening already considerable youth budgets. Once again, the distribution of finance and opportunity is being dictated by the few.

We are resorting back to a system that has failed Scotland resulting in our exclusion from the final stages of international tournaments for 20 years. We have relied on clubs to produce talent but they have not produced the pipeline we expected and as a result, it makes no sense to go down the same road again. The idea of the Regional Academies will help overcome the chronic weaknesses in our current talent development programme and put the interests of the country above the narrow interests of the clubs. The clubs have their own ambitions and needs, which must be met, but this does not necessarily equate with the needs of our national side. We are in danger of squandering a once-in-a-generation opportunity to reshape youth development, of both sexes. These are important factors especially when the women's game holds out so much promise and potential and is likely an integral and mainstream part of our future thinking.

Football DNA is to be found everywhere in Scotland, not just in our cities. Any new strategy must treat talented young people like gold-dust. These young people are our football capital, which, if properly invested in, will provide the basis of future football success. But wastage rates are high and the pathway for young people is fraught with challenges. Young people need to keep their career options open and maintain their links with education. A better distribution of opportunities will help address those concerns. Clubs, despite their obvious interest in young players, are not providing enough opportunities for them to play at the highest level. There are too many average foreign players being imported into our game and there are too few incentives for clubs to play young players. Short-termism dominates instead of long-term thinking. There was a time, especially during the 'Golden Age', that if you were good enough, you were old enough. It is difficult to understand why this has changed. What needs to be done?

- Project Brave must be revisited and revised;

- We should stop financing clubs that are well financed and instead spread the resource to involve and reward others;

- We must proceed with the idea of establishing a network of Regional Academies throughout Scotland with the 42 clubs having some access and being able, in some form, to participate. The focus of our interest must be talented young people, not the clubs. While many of the clubs will have their own facilities, they must see themselves part of the national drive and fit into the national football plan;

- Clubs should be part of the national set up, but not dominate, and be able to work closely with the Regional Academies;

- Similar to other countries, the whole of Scotland must have access to first class facilities;

- Schools should be open for sport every day of the year; there can be no excuse for wasting valuable public facilities and seeing them closed for long parts of the school year. In the national interest and for a number of health and fitness reasons, access to facilities should be made affordable to many families and children who find accessing them increasingly out of their reach;

- A good start has been made to improve facilities, but more needs to be done in partnership with local councils and the Scottish Government;

- The delivery of our youth and elite strategy must engage outside interests and extend the level of expertise available to the football authorities;

- Incentives must be made available to clubs to encourage more opportunities for young Scots;

- Schools must now be invited to play a more prominent role in youth policy;

- The percentage of Scots in the Scottish Premiership must be increased;

- The Academy structure should be wholly financed by the SFA and not be subject to the lack of resources in any part of Scotland. This is, after all, a national project. Football politics must give way to common sense;

- The youth players pathway, access to continuing education and child protection measures need to be transformed;

- The women's game must become an integral part of the Academy structure. It was originally part of the concept but appears to have been taken out. This should be the most important priority in Scottish football. The clubs have not delivered and we must not repeat the mistakes of the past. Scotland needs a different path to success. Long-term thinking requires us to look more holistically at every aspect of national talent needs and international success.

Integrated Setup

Our coach/manager setup, the women's game, the national team, the performance director, the different age groups that participate in international football and the youth development and elite talent must be more effectively coordinated, and also be given the level of resource consistent with a new and more ambitious role on the international stage. The turnover of Scottish managers and performance directors reveals a telling commentary on the lack of continuity, consistency and long-term thinking.

There must be more urgency. Nearly one decade on from my review, we still do not have a settled elite structure. This is worrying and damaging. Unless these outstanding matters can be resolved and we can pin down a successful way of proceeding, there is a good case for an independent inquiry into Project Brave and outstanding issue of youth and elite talent. There are serious problems surrounding the pathway for young players, and the human and children's rights that should be protected. Some progress has been made, but not enough. The Children's Commissioner and the government have been vocal on these matters. The game thinks the government is meddling in their affairs, while the government thinks the game is dragging its feet. This again illustrates the point that football must not think it operates out with the norms and values of modern society.

5. Fans and Government

The game in its present form remains insular, hesitant in its dealings with the outside world and remarkably defensive about its operations. This behaviour generates unnecessary criticism, distorts the game's identity and creates barriers for those who wish to help. Fans and government are vital for the realisation of a national football plan and for generating the good will and support to make it happen. Fans are invaluable; a precious resource and the main stay of the game. Many clubs are clinging on to their traditional support but there is a need to widen the support base by attracting children, young people, women, girls and families. Improving the fan offering at this level would help. While money is a constraint on improving facilities, the football authorities could be doing more to assist individual clubs by giving them a priority in the pooling of national resources and at the centre, relieving clubs of matters that could be dealt with at national level.

At the national level of the game, fans should be involved in decision-making, policy-making, monitoring the game and also be part of the drive to modernise football.

Government presents a different proposition. They are involved in the game in so many ways and if given the opportunity, could do more. The government should play a bigger role in the development of a National Football Plan and be able to help in significant ways. The relationship between them must improve with the game being more open and willing to be more transparent in its dealings. Government shouldn't be perceived as political. There is a great deal of mistrust and, at times, ignorance of what each other is doing. The government has sponsored the League Cup, a considerable investment of taxpayer's money, and are also involved in supporting youth development, anti-racism and sectarianism work, financing of facilities and helping fans organisations. Given the right conditions, government could do a great deal to advance the ambitions set out in my vision for the future of the game. But the game must respond. Health and fitness do not sit comfortably with betting and gambling; the government needs to be convinced its commitment to the game will not be compromised.

On the bigger stage, Scotland will be able to emulate the achievements of small countries like Denmark, Uruguay, Sweden, Croatia and Iceland if we can harness positive help from the wider Scotland, especially the Scottish Government and Parliament. At the same time, we can ensure our fans are more constructively engaged in shaping the future of their game, a game they finance, support, defend, criticise and eternally worry about. There should be a much bigger role for our 32 local councils, working in partnership with the game to secure greater success.

6. Being Part of a Sporting Revolution

The final priority links football, in a more ambitious way, to the sporting revolution in Scotland, urgently needed to make our country fitter and better able to tackle some of the massive health problems facing adults and young people in our society. In partnership with other sports, we must involve more people in grassroots participation and vastly increase the numbers. Inequality is a striking characteristic of poor health and fitness. Obesity is growing to dangerous levels. Physical Education in schools is being constrained by curriculum pressures. Football is remarkably well-placed to work in partnership with government to achieve this revolution. Urgency is the key and finance is essential.

An Effective Structure/Organisation

My narrative has the made the case for a radical approach to renew football in Scotland and create the conditions for a new golden era. I have identified key challenges, ideas, themes, principals, and priorities that could transform the game. But there is one important part of this football jigsaw puzzle to put in place: the structure or organisation that could take this forward.

Long-Term Decline

Accepting the complexity of interpreting decline, my analysis suggests we focus on four major components. First, institutions and organisations failed to understand or respond to the end of our 'Golden Era' in the mid-90s. Second, the creation of the Scottish Premier League and its links to money, broadcasting and the financial pressures on clubs in the early part of the new millennium dramatically altered the football landscape. Third, the international game disappeared off the radar screen. Finally, the politics of inevitability kicked in. Within the ruling bodies of the game, there was no challenge to what was happening and the interests of the few dominated.

The Politics of Inevitability

The politics of inevitability and the politics of eternity have become important ways of describing the process where organisations can be influenced and conditioned to a point where they are overwhelmed by change and simply see no alternative to what is happening. This is often accompanied by the politics of eternity where a preoccupation with sentiment, nostalgia, and, sometimes, delusion about the past provides great memories and history, but little or no incentive to recreate them or learn lessons. The politics of inevitability and eternity are dangerous, especially when they become convenient and reassuring substitutes for change and a comfortable escape from a game that very few people think is achieving or performing.

How Many Organisations?

The number of organisation running Scottish football has always been a source of debate. There were three until the Scottish Football League merged with the Scottish Premiere League to become the Scottish Professional Football League and since then, with some justification, there has been a body of opinion, which has argued for further reform including the merging of the SFA and the SPFL/SP. My case for change suggests this would make little sense. Any merger based on the current state of the game, would see the club game expand its power, authority and territory at the expense of the wider game, the youth strategy and our national sides at all levels. The rebalancing of the game can only be assured by seeing it through the prism of a dominant position being established for the national game. The SFA has to contend with a Professional Game Board, a Non-Professional Game Board operating at the heart of their decision-making as well as the SPFL, including the Scottish Premiership, having their own organisation. The SFA and its priorities and needs, the common good of the game and the ambitions of the wider game are lost in a structure that is dominated by overlapping committees, overlapping memberships, the same agendas and an over representation of SPFL and SP members in matters that are primarily the preserve of the SFA. The current structure of decision-making and policy formulation at the Hampden HQ is heavily weighted against the SFA and in favour of the club game, which can manifest itself through a structure that is no longer appropriate for the wider needs of the game. This must be changed. Any new ideas about how the game should be run, must acknowledge three other considerations.

First, it can't be said often enough, that membership organisations are notoriously difficult to change. FIFA and UEFA are fiercely protective of their historic commitment to membership and in so many ways this is a good thing. But the problem has become one of balancing organisational efficiency, coherent and effective decision-making, relevance and modernity with securing maximum membership involvement, real democracy and members being able to contribute to policy formulation. Traditions, customs, conventions and procedures are all rightly part of Scotland's football heritage, however modernity sometimes struggles to make a breakthrough. One thing has always puzzled me: the process for electing the President of the SFA. Where else would you find an important appointment based on the question of time served, movement through the ranks and good old type military considerations? As the President and Vice-President serve on, or chair, most of the committees, this becomes an important issue; perhaps less about substance and more about symbolism, but still relevant.

Second, other countries, and operating under similar UEFA constraints, have faced similar problems but have managed to achieve a better balance between club and national game and, as a result, have done much better in international tournaments. Clearly, there are multiple factors operating in each of the associations world-wide, with very different social, economic, cultural and political contexts, so it is often difficult to assess how factors interrelate with each other.

Third, other sports in the United Kingdom have restructured their organisations with a view to reshaping their membership organisations to meet the challenges of increasing competition but none of them seem to be facing the complete imbalances and distorted priorities that bedevil Scottish football. They have made changes based on giving a higher prominence to the national game, more involvement for their members through an effective use of Councils or Congresses and the restructuring of directorates to emphasise the importance of performance, youth development and grass-roots participation.

A New Structure

My personal football journey is nearly at an end. I have attempted to make the case for a football renaissance in Scotland built on the positive examples and experiences I have found elsewhere; where countries have marked themselves out for special attention as a result of the progress they have made. Adjusting to modern day challenges, having a balanced agenda and priorities for their national game and being ruthlessly ambitious are the key qualities. These countries have put their national imprint on a modern game that demands extraordinarily high levels of commitment.

Different countries, at different times, in different circumstances and for different reasons have turned their games around after setbacks. Others have arrived for the first time, over the last few years, in the final stages of international tournaments despite the odds being stacked against them. Russia 2018 has also revealed amazing performances by countries like Croatia, losing out to a superior French side in the final of the World cup. Scotland seems out of step with the football world in which we seem incapable or unwilling to change or accept the challenges that other countries have taken in their stride.

A new structure or organisation is needed to unify the game. Its supreme task will be to confront a football landscape that is scarred by a series of home-made fault lines that are damaging our game and resulting in Scotland falling further behind.

The Triumph of Excellence over Feuding Factions

Sporting power and finance versus sporting excellence; Club versus country; Game versus fans; politics of inevitability versus politics of change; narrow or vested interests versus the common good; SPFL versus the SFA; game resentment versus government frustration; and while it has added a bit of drama, it does describe the core of the problem, the few versus the many.

Features of a New Organisation

Scottish football must escape from its immediate past and start to deliver on much needed reforms. But we must go further and establish a new organisation/structure if we want a genuine renaissance which restores national pride and rebuilds our credibility, at both club and country level and on the international stage.

The structure is roughly illustrated in the flow chart and highlights extensive changes and new ways of working. It emphasises the primacy of the game, which is bigger than the sum of its parts and free from the vested interests ruling the game at the present time. It confirms that rebalancing the game will result in the SFA becoming the one body and the one board in Scottish football that will oversee the national game, give it direction, long-term thinking, strategic resource allocation and include a significant proportion of interests from outside the game. The labyrinth of committees – overlapping membership and agendas – making up the present SFA structure will disappear and real power and authority will be vested in the SFA. This will provide streamlining and will halt the policy and territorial aggrandisement of the SPFL, and especially the Scottish Premiership. Football will be coming home to the SFA! I am sorry I couldn't resist the opportunity.

The Structure of Scottish Football

Today – The Present

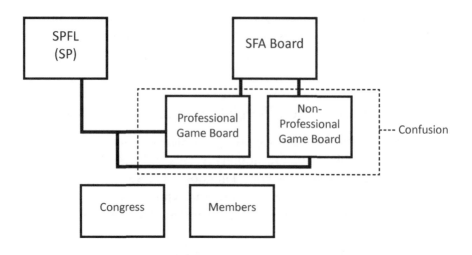

Tomorrow – The Future

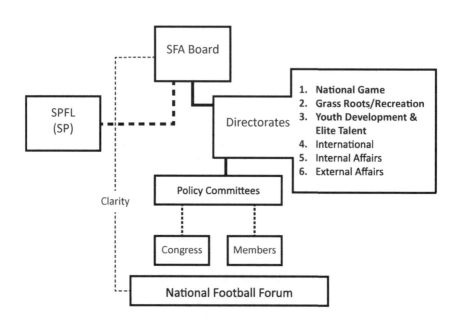

The SPFL, including the SP, will carry on and while remaining autonomous as they are at present, they will not be able to overwhelm SFA committees or dictate wider game policy but instead, will be involved and consulted on relevant matters. The SPFL and the SP cannot have their cake and eat someone else's. The SPFL has vital work to do, but as repeated often, not at the expense of the wider game. The SPFL will be represented on the SFA Board. The Members Organisation is currently in the hands of the few and requires an effective role and a sense of purpose. It has been pointed out earlier that it is a membership organisation in name only. In addition to having a say at AGM's, the members should be able to have a more effective input to policy and, when necessary, the opportunity for their Congress to establish committees in a similar manner to the Scottish Parliament. These would help advise both the SFA and the SPFL on current topics and long-term thinking. This role would be innovative and strictly advisory. This would encourage more outside interest and involvement. Members must be able to have a real say in decision making, unburdened by a medieval voting system which smacks of Russian and Chinese elections where democracy means voting for or against one candidate. President Trump would describe this as a 'rigged system'. Football would still be run by its membership, but in a totally different and meaningful way.

At the heart of the SFA, there should be more clarity on lines of accountability and responsibility as well as more effective signalling of outcomes and reasoning at the heart of decision-making. Removing the grip of the SPFL/SP should help. The SFA should consist of identifiable Directorates responsible for informing the SFA Board, receiving policy information from the Congress or members and executing and delivering outcomes. There is a myriad of internal functions being carried out which are vital for the functioning of the game – let's call them internal affairs in a new set up – but to deal with government, fans and the wider Scotland, we should create an external affairs directorate to emphasise that the game is connecting and is seeking ways to become more accountable to the public, and more responsive to its needs.

And way behind the other possible changes in terms of importance, the game could establish a National Football Forum to allow the rest of Scotland to participate and have an opportunity to be updated on current thinking and new ideas. It would be purely consultative, but helpful to a game that has drifted away from its historical origins, its faithful fans and along suffering public.

Renaissance it is!

Football success can be ours, I have no doubt about that. It is our choice to make but a generation on from our 'Golden Age', we have shown little interest in taking the decisions necessary to turn the game around. A cursory glance at the demise of the game reveals we have no excuses left and face the brutal truth that in Club competitions, we cannot win success at the highest level in Europe and internationally. We are no longer making any impact in the European Championships or in the World Cup. Despite the drift from the priorities of the national game and focus on the Scottish Premiership, our senior clubs have fared little better than the national side. I should add that the women's game is doing well. Qualifying for the European Championships in 2017 was a tremendous achievement and there is the prospect of the team qualifying for the World cup in 2019. We are poised to make great strides in the women's game and our support for their efforts must be stepped up.

A new and powerful voice is needed at the heart of Scottish football. This must be a reinvigorated SFA, with an agenda for change.

It is however, Scotland's choice to make! But whatever happens, we need a debate.

My parting shot refers to a comment from journalist, Simon Kuper, writing 'Globalisation 1 – Nationalism 0'. This article in the *Financial Times Magazine* talked about the success of the World Cup in Russia. But, in a characteristically skeptical manner, he was talking about the good behaviour of the fans and said,

> It's the fifth peaceable World Cup in a row. England's fans in Nizhny Novgorod last weekend chanted nothing more aggressive than, 'Are you watching Scotland?'

These comments from supporters of the historic 'Auld Enemy' said it all. They were there, and we weren't. How many times Scotland, do we have to be at the humorous but sharp end of ridicule and derision? I am tired of it, how about you?

Chronology

1424   Earliest historical reference to 'fute-ball' in Scotland; James I outlawed the playing of the game in the 'Football Act 1424'.

1863   The game starts to gain popularity in Scotland following first rules of association football being established in London by the FA.

1867   Formation of Queen's Park – Scotland's longest established football club.

1872   First international game between Scotland and England.

1873   Scottish Football Association is formed.
First major competition – 'The Scottish Cup'.

1882   Scottish Football Association agree on uniform set of rules.

1883   British Home Championship established – UK home nations.

1887   SFA instructs all of their teams to withdraw from the FA.

1890   Scottish Football League is founded.

1893   Professional Football is officially recognized by the SFA.

1910   The SFA joins FIFA, the international governing body for association football.

1929   Scotland's first game against a non-UK country (Norway).

1954   Scotland competes in first major tournament – FIFA World Cup.

1956   Hibernian reach the semi-finals of the European Cup.

1958   Scotland qualifies for final stages of the World Cup in 1958 and subsequently in 1974, 1978, 1982, 1986, 1990 and 1998.
The SFA joins UEFA, the administrative body for association football in Europe.

1960   Real Madrid beat Eintracht Frankfurt 7-3 at Hampden Park, Glasgow where 127,000 people watched what is widely believed to be the greatest football match ever.

1966   England wins the FIFA World Cup at Wembley Stadium.

1967   Celtic become the first British team to win the European Cup.
Scotland win 3-2 against England in the final stages of the 1966-67 British Home Championship.

1967   Aberdeen play their first official match in competitive European football in the 1967 European Cup Winners Cup.

1972   The Scottish Women's Football Association is formed.

1972   Rangers win European Cup Winners Cup.

1978   Scotland qualifies for the FIFA World Cup in Argentina.

1984   Ayrshire-born Rose Reilly captains A.C Milan. She led Italy to win the (then unofficial) Women's World Cup.

1992   Qualified for UEFA European Championships.

1996   Qualified for UEFA European Championships.

1998   Qualified for FIFA World Cup in France.
        Scottish Premier League is formed.

2013   The Scottish Professional Football League is formed as part of a general reconstruction.

2009   SFA commissions Henry McLeish to undertake a major review of Scottish football.

2010   Review of Scottish football is published.

2017   Scotland's women's national team qualify for their first major tournament – UEFA Women's Euro.

Bibliography and References

Accounts Commission, "Physical recreation services in local government" Audit Scotland, 2010.

Ahmed, Murad and Massoudi Arash, "FIFA Faces clash over Plans for Global Football", FT Weekend, 2018

Archdiocese of Washington, "The eight stages of the rise and fall of civilisations", Life Site. 2016.

Arnott, Walter, "A few incidents in Association Football", scottishsporthistory.com 1876

BBC Home, "Jock Stein Dies 1985", bbc.co.uk/Scotland/sportsscotland 1985

BBC news, "Scottish football, a cause of sectarianism", bbc.com/news/uk-scotland. 2015.

BBC Scotland, "11 Surprising Facts", Scotland's Game, 2016

BBC Scotland, "Scotland's Game", TV Series about the Role of Football in Scottish Society (four documentaries), 2016

BBC Sort Football, "How women's football battled for survival", news.bbc.co.uk 2005.

BBC Sport, "SPFL reports 12 % increase in match attendances for 2016-17", bbc.com/sport/football 2017.

BBC, "Children's commissioner warning on football child exploitation", bbc.com/news/uk-scotland. 2016

Berry, Graham, "Gordon Strachan's genetics theory doesn't stand up and 2010 World Cup Final proves that says Mark Wotte" Daily Record 2017

Boutros, Tristan, "10 principles that promote good governance", processexcellencenetwork.com 2015

Bradley, "The Undercurrents of Scottish Football", Wiley Online Library. 1997

Bradley, Joseph M. "Football in Scotland: a history of Political and Ethnic identity", The International Journey of the History of Sport. 2007

Bradley, Joseph, "Political, religious and cultural identities: the undercurrents of Scottish football", Political Studies Association. Onlinelibrary.wiley.com 2007.

Brownstone, Jordana, "The Bosman Ruling-Impact of player mobility on FIFA rankings", Haverford College, Economics Department. 2010.

BundesligaFanatic, "1960 European Cup Final", bundesligafanatic.com

Butcher, Michael, "PFA FERS Malaja, the New Bosman", The Guardian. 1999.

Collins, Jim, "Good to Great", Random House Business Books. 2001.

Conn, David, "Football's biggest issue: the struggle facing boys rejected by academies", The Guardian. 2017.

Conn, David, "How can football clubs capture the social value of the beautiful game", The Guardian. 2010

Currie, David, "SFA to choose between Hampden and Murrayfield as home of Scottish football", bbc.com/sport/football. 2018.

D.D.Bone, "Scottish Football Reminiscences and Sketches", John Menzies & Co. 1890

Deloitte, "Ahead of the curve-Annual Review of Football Finance", Sports business group, 2017.

Dick, WM, "The rules of the Scottish Football association", Weatherston & Son Glasgow 1875.

Doidge, Mark, "Fan involvement in football clubs: the German Model", The Football Federation. 2014.

Donegan, Lawrence, "Nothing compares to the raw and rugged brilliance of Scottish football", The Guardian, 2018

Easton, Craig, 'The Future of Scottish Football', Blueprint for Football .com. 2012

EPFL, "EPFL presents its new fan attendance report", Association of European Football Leagues. 2018.

Espiner, Tom, "Sky and BT win premier league TV rights", bbc.com/news/uk 2018

European Commission, "Sport, youth fitness and physical activity", eacea.ec.europe.eu/national-policies 2017

European Football Championship, "All Time Table", European -football -statistics.co.uk 2012.

Ewing, Forsyth, Ogden and Newport, "England v Scotland; Greta Moments from the past", Telegraph. 2013

Farrey, Tom, "The critical role of sports in society", aspeninstitute.org/blogposts 2012.

FIFA, "History of football-Britain, the home of football", fifa.com 2018

Football Association England, "The FA Structure", 2015

Football Bible, "Top 10 football stadium disasters", football-bible.com/soccer-info top 2016.

Football History, "The history of football", footballhistory.org 2018.

Forsyth, Roddy, "The decline of Scottish Football will not dampen the enthusiasm of the Tartan army", The Telegraph. 2016

Gates, Philip, "Five Reasons why Scottish football is in good health", Business Insider, insider.co.uk 2018

Gibbons, Glenn, "SOS Scotland: is there a way back for a once great footballing nation?", The Guardian. 2009

Global Team events, "Soccer in Italy-A look at the Culture and history of Italy's most popular sport", global events.com/soccer undated

Gordon, Mark, "Scotland Manager Wanted: Pride, Passion and Genetics". All out Football. 2018

Graham, John and Amos, Bruce and Plumptre, Tim, "Principles of good governance", Institute of Governance. 2003.

Grahame, Ewing, "Opening the 1998 World Cup against Brazil was huge", Daily Record. 2014

Greer, Germaine, "Football counts as culture just as much as opera", The Guardian, 2008.

Hall, Tom, "Scotland in 1998: Open with a bang and close with a Whimper", The Scottish Football Blog. 2010

Harris Rob, "Meeting with England highlights decline of Scottish Soccer", Seattle Times. 2016

Harris, Nick, "Revealed; The most dedicated football nations", www.sport intelligence.com. 2012

Harrison, Jody, "Scottish football finances in order". Evening Times. 2015.

Hassan, David and Hamil, Sean, "Models of football governance and management in international sport", Soccer and Society, 2010

Hassan, Gerry, "Why does football matter so much/ And is it about something else?", Scottish Review. 2016.

Herron, Lyndsay, "Ex-Celtic and Rangers players on short-list for SFA Exec job", Scotsman, 2018

House of Commons, "Culture, Media and Sport Committee publishes report on football governance", www.parliament.uk 2011

House of Commons. "Culture, Media and Sport Committee-Seventh report-Football governance", 2011.

Hytner, David, " Ronaldo's stunning overhead kick helps real Madrid floor Juventus", The Guardian. 2018.

International Olympic Committee, "Basic universal principles of good governance of the Olympic and sports movement", Seminar, 2008.

Jackson, Jamie, "How Dutch seeds can help England's grassroots youth football to grow", The Guardian. 2011.

Jackson, Jamie, "The Munich disaster 60 years on: They were the best team by far", The Guardian, 2018

Jackson, Keith, "Scottish football's pathetic TV deal is bottom of the Euro table", Daily Record, 2017

Johnson, Greg, "What has Scottish Football ever done for us". Thefalsenine.co.uk, 2012

Kane, Paul, "Bosman transfer ruling stunted Scottish game", BBC sport, bbc.com/sport 2015

Karon, Tony, "What soccer means to the world", Time. 2004

Katzenbach, Oelschlegel, Thomas James, "10 principles of organisational culture", strategy-business.com 2016

Lee Simon, "Common Good", Britannica.com 2012.

Levesque, Roger, "Celtic v Rangers; Catholicism v Protestantism", Stanford.edu/class. 2002.

Liew, Jonathan, "How the Bosman rule changed football for ever", The Telegraph. 2015.

Linklater, John, "Old Firm remain in a league of their own", The Herald, 1996.

Llyr, Owain, "Welsh football: Leagues restructure confirmed by FAW", BBC Wales Sport, bbc.com/sport/football 2017.

MacDonald, Matthew, "What led to the rise and decline of Football in Scotland", Quora, 2016

MacDonald, Paul, BBC, "Scotland Open the World Cup 1998", A Sporting Nation, 1998

MacDonald, Ronnie, "How Scottish fans are taking charge in an increasingly polarised global market", the conversation.com 2016.

MacPherson, Graeme, "State of Scottish football: does the TV deal represent value for money?", The Herald. 2015.

Marlon, Brandon, "The decline and fall of modern civilisation", the Algemeiner, 2015.

McArdle, Helen, "Health of Children in Scotland, among worst in Europe", The Herald, 2017,

McCall, Chris, "How much are Scotland's football clubs worth", The Scotsman. 2015.

McDowell, Matthew, "Scottish Football and Popular Culture", Scottish Leisure History Blog. 2013

McIlvanney Hugh, "The Football men revisited", Three- part documentary, Busby, Stein and Shankly. 1997.

McKenna, Kevin, "At least Scotland's women know how to play football", The Guardian. 2018.

McLaughlin, Chris, "Scottish clubs set for vote on league reconstruction proposals", BBC Sport, 2013.

McLean, David, "Scotland's all- time record football attendances", Scotsman. 2017

McLeish, Henry, "Review of Scottish Football, Part 2 -Football's choice-facing the future-Governance, Leadership and Structures", 2010.

McLeish, Henry, "Pride, passion and perseverance; what next for Scottish football", Sunday Mail. 2018

McLeish, Henry, "Review of Scottish Football, Part 1-The Grassroots, Recreation and youth development-Facing the Future", 2010

McLeish, Henry, "Scottish football: renaissance and recriminations", Scotsman. 2018

McLeish, Henry, "Search for Success key to football future, Scotsman. 2018

McPartlin Patrick, "Scottish Football Attendances, Highest in Europe", Scotsman, 2018

Miller, Julianna & Silverman, Brian, "Soccer culture in the US", sites.duke.edu/wcwp/tournament 2014

Mitchell, Andy, "Football described by giants of the game", John Leng &co., London and Dundee, 1904.

Moore, Glenn, "Scots on the Rocks; What's gone wrong north of the border?", The Independent. 2011.

Morrow, Stephen, "Scottish football-It's a funny old business", Journal of Sports economics. 2006.

Murray, Ewan, "Its time for the SPL to open its doors to the Scottish Leagues best", The Guardian. 2010.

Murray, Ewan, 'Pitches, Coaches and iPads; what are the reasons for Scotland's talent decline', The Guardian, 2016

Murray, Ewan, 2Emotion, history, politics, money and the great Hampden head-scratcher", The Guardian. 2018.

National Gambling Helpline, "Be gamble aware, to get help when you need it", football-stadiums. co.uk/articles

NHS Health Scotland, "Children and Health inequalities", healthscotland.scot/population. 2018.

NHS Health Scotland, "Employment inequality", healthscotland.scot/health-inequalities, 2018

NHS Health Scotland, "Measuring health inequalities", healthscotland.scot/health-inequalities 2018

No Name, "Five famous Scottish nights to rival Celtic's victory", Telegraph, 2012.

No Name, "Football, Fire and Ice: the inside story of Iceland's remarkable rise", The Guardian. 2016

No Name, "The death of Scottish Football", Blog. The Football Life.co.uk

No Name, "The early beginnings of Scottish football; Popularity amid violence", Soccer Politics, A discussion Forum.

Paterson, Stewart, "Thatcher to blame for Scotland not qualifying for World Cup says Sir Alex Ferguson", Evening Times. 2015.

Rainbow, Jamie, "Scottish Football; Where did it all go wrong", world soccer .com. 2011

Reeve, Sarah, "The beautiful game; why does football inspire such a passion around the world?", DeerParkHPE, 2009.

Reid, Carlton, "Cycling is bigger in Scotland than football, says new report", Cycling Scotland, bike-biz.com/news 2018.

Responsible and Safe Gambling, "Football's relationship with betting and gambling industry in the UK", football-stadiums.co.uk/articles 2017.

Royal Netherlands Football Association, " Dutch Football history and Structure", KNVB. 2018.

Rudge, David, "Great Scot! Where have all Scotland's good players gone?". The Independent. 2012.

Russell, Grant, "25 years on: remembering the Scottish Super League", stv.tv/sport/football

Scotti, Dan, "More than a game: what actually makes soccer so important to people all over the world", elitedaily.com 2014

Scottish FA, "Annual Review-2017"

Scottish FA, "Brief History of the SFA", web.archive.org/web 2018

Scottish FA, "Hampden park host venue for UEFA Euro 2020", Scotland United, 2017.

Scottish FA, "Scottish Football Board and Committees" 2018.

Scottish Football Monitor, "Scottish Football Administration in the 21st Century". Sfm.scot/

Scottish Football Supporters Association, "Transforming Scottish Football- The Fans Manifesto" 2016.

Scottish Government, "A more active Scotland-building a legacy from the Commonwealth Games", beta.gov.scot/publications 2014.

Scottish Government, "Headline indicators of health inequalities", beta.gov.scot/publications 2018

Scottish Government, "Physical Activity and Sport", beta.gov.scot/policies/physical-activity 2018.

Scottish Government, "Religion in Scotland and perceptions of the extent of sectarianism", gov.scot/publications 2015

Scottish Rugby, "Inspiring Scotland through Rugby-Scottish Rugby Structure-Scottish Rugby PLC Board", scottishrugby.org 2016

Scottish Sporting Anthology, "Digitised books and articles", scottishsporthistory.com

Settle, Michael, "How Thatcher's government pulled the plug on the new Hampden", The Herald. 2017.

SFA, Financial Report, Commercial review, Marketing Communications, Scotland Supporters Club, 2016

Shobe, Hunter, "Place, identity and football: Catalonia, Catalanisme and football club Barcelona, 1899-1975", tandfonline .com 2008.

Skidelsky, Robert, "Is Western civilisation in Terminal Decline", The Guardian. 2015.

Sky Football news, "SPL clubs back revamp", skysports.com/football news. 2013.

Smith, Chris, "What is happening to Scottish Football", Huffington Post. 2014

Soccer Politics, "The Old Firm: Scotland's claim to football fame", duke.edu/wcwp/research-projects/Scotland 2018

Social Issues Research centre, "Football Passions", Commissioned research. 1997.

Speirs Graham, "The Decline of Scotland as an International Football Team", The Herald, 2012

Spence, Jim, "Can big crowds ever return to Scottish football", Blog. Bbc.co.uk/blogs/jimspence 2012.

Spence, Jim, "Plans for Scottish League reform will see stadium rules relaxed". BBC, 2013.

Spencer, Stuart, "Women's football in Scotland", Scottish Football Museum, 2017

SPFL, "SPFL attendances soar in 2016/17", spfl.co.uk 2017.

Spiers, Graham, "Spiers on sport; battered and bruised, Scottish football is still a fine thing", The Herald. 2015

Sport Scotland, "Community Sports Hubs 2016/17 headline figures", 2017.

Sports Mail reporter, "Bill Shankly: the top 10 quotes of a Liverpool legend", Daily Mail. 2009.

Stone, Martin, "Scottish Football's Crisis of Confidence", The Unmodern Man. 2008

Suter, Keith, "The importance of sport in society", global directions.com 2017.

Symon, John, "Why is football so popular in Scotland if they're so bad at it", Quora, Blog. 2017

Symon, Ken, "Insider Football Finance Index is a new measure of Scottish football club success", Business Insider, 2017.

Taylor, Daniel, "Liverpool's stunning first half salvo leave Manchester City's hope on the rocks", The Guardian. 2018.

Titford, Richard, "Three of a kind-McIlvanney's tribute to a trio of famous managers", When Saturday comes. Wsc.co.uk 1997.

Townsend, Jon, "The Icelandic Football Model", The Football Times. 2015.

UEFA, "European Qualifiers for UEFA EURO 2020: how it works", uefa.com 2017.

UEFA, "UEFA Nations League 2018/19 League Phase Draw", uefa.com 2018.

Velasquez, Andre, Shanks, S.J., and Michael J Meyer, "The Common Good, Issues in Ethics" 2014.

Waddell, Gordon, "SFA needs independent thinkers to hold Stewart Regan accountable and turn around a sinking ship", Sunday Mail. 2018.

Walters, Geoff and Tacon, Richard, "Corporate Social responsibility in European Football: models of football governance", UEFA Research Grant Programme, 2011.

Watkins, Michael D.2What is organisational Culture? And why should we care? Harvard Business Review. 2013.

Wickstream, Mads A., "Council of Europe report calls for stronger governance reforms in sport", Play the Game.org 2018.

Wikipedia, "1998 FIFA World Cup Group A".

Wikipedia, "Iceland national football team", Wikipedia.org

Wikipedia, "Northern Ireland national football team", Wikipedia.org

Wikipedia, "Republic of Ireland national football team", Wikipedia.org.

Wikipedia, "Scotland at the FIFA World Cup", Wikipedia.org 2018

Wikipedia, "Scotland at the UEFA European Championship"

Wikipedia, "Scottish football attendance Records", en.wikipedia.org/wiki/Scottish 2018.

Wikipedia, "Uruguay national football team, wikepedia.org

Wikipedia, "Wales National Football Team", Wikipedia.org

Wikipedia, "Women's football in Scotland", Wikipedia.org.uk 2018.

Wilson, Fraser, "The alarming decline of Scottish clubs in European Competitions laid bare", Daily Record. 2017

Wilson, Richard, "Why Scottish bosses are in a league of their own", The Independent, 2011.

Women's History Scotland, "The history of women's football in Scotland", womenhistoryscotland.org 2017.

Wren, David, "Hugh McIlvanney believes the decline of Scottish Football is irreversible", Daily Record. 2016

Luath Press Limited

committed to publishing well written books worth reading

LUATH PRESS takes its name from Robert Burns, whose little collie
Luath (*Gael.*, swift or nimble) tripped up Jean Armour at a wedding
and gave him the chance to speak to the woman who was to be his wife
and the abiding love of his life. Burns called one of the 'Twa Dogs'
Luath after Cuchullin's hunting dog in Ossian's *Fingal*.
Luath Press was established in 1981 in the heart of
Burns country, and is now based a few steps up
the road from Burns' first lodgings on
Edinburgh's Royal Mile. Luath offers you
distinctive writing with a hint of
unexpected pleasures.
Most bookshops in the UK, the US, Canada,
Australia, New Zealand and parts of Europe,
either carry our books in stock or can order them
for you. To order direct from us, please send a £sterling
cheque, postal order, international money order or your
credit card details (number, address of cardholder and
expiry date) to us at the address below. Please add post
and packing as follows: UK – £1.00 per delivery address;
overseas surface mail – £2.50 per delivery address; overseas airmail –
£3.50 for the first book to each delivery address, plus £1.00 for each
additional book by airmail to the same address. If your order is a gift,
we will happily enclose your card or message at no extra charge.

Luath Press Limited
543/2 Castlehill
The Royal Mile
Edinburgh EH1 2ND
Scotland
Telephone: +44 (0)131 225 4326 (24 hours)
email: sales@luath. co.uk
Website: www. luath.co.uk